AF484463

Preparation For The King Series: Esther, A Study of Self-Care, Faith and Victory

Ann Marie Thrives

ISBN: 979-8-9894811-2-5 - Softcover
ISBN: 979-8-9894811-3-2 - ebook

Comfort Print

All Scriptures quoted or referenced are taken from the KJV, NKJV and other various authorized and free versions.

REIGNITING PASSION

A Husband's Guide to Strengthening Intimacy

WELLNESS WHISPERER

CONTENTS

INTRODUCTION

In the journey of marriage, couples often encounter periods where the flames of passion may flicker, and the once palpable intimacy feels elusive. However, the beauty of a committed relationship lies in the ability to reignite that spark and deepen the connection between partners. This guide is crafted for husbands seeking to enhance the intimacy in their marriage, offering practical and heartfelt suggestions to bring back the warmth, joy, and passion that initially bound them together.

Navigating the complexities of modern life can sometimes lead to neglecting the very foundation of a strong and loving relationship. Through effective communication, shared experiences, and intentional gestures, husbands can actively contribute to the renewal of passion in their marriages. This guide will explore various aspects of fostering intimacy, from the power of open communication to the importance of shared dreams and the role of both emotional and physical connection.

As you embark on this journey to strengthen the bond with your spouse, remember that small, consistent efforts often yield profound results. Whether it's surprising your partner with thoughtful gestures, prioritizing quality time together, or rekindling the romance that brought you two together, the commitment to reigniting passion is a shared endeavor.

This guide aims to inspire and guide husbands in fostering an environment where love, understanding, and desire can flourish. By embracing these principles, you can set the stage for a deeper, more meaningful connection with your spouse, ultimately creating a marriage that continues to thrive and evolve over time.

Chapter 1
UNDERSTANDING THE DYNAMICS OF INTIMACY

Intimacy is the cornerstone of a fulfilling and enduring marriage. It goes beyond physical closeness; it encompasses emotional, intellectual, and spiritual connection. To reignite passion, husbands must delve into the intricate dynamics of intimacy, recognizing the multifaceted aspects that contribute to a strong and vibrant relationship.

Emotional Intimacy:

- Emotional intimacy involves sharing one's innermost thoughts and feelings. It requires vulnerability and trust.

- Cultivate a safe space where both partners feel comfortable expressing themselves without fear of judgment.

Effective Communication:

- Communication is the bridge to understanding. Husbands should actively listen, show empathy, and communicate their own emotions openly.

- Practice both verbal and non-verbal communication to strengthen emotional connection.

Intellectual Connection:

- Engage in stimulating conversations that go beyond day-to-day routines. Discuss shared interests, ideas, and future plans.

- Intellectual intimacy enhances mutual respect and admiration for each other's minds.

Physical Intimacy:

- Beyond the sexual aspect, physical intimacy includes non-sexual touch, cuddling, and gestures of affection.

- Discover each other's love languages and incorporate them into your daily interactions.

Spiritual Bond:

- For some couples, spirituality plays a significant role in intimacy. This might involve shared beliefs, values, or practices.

- Connect on a spiritual level by participating in activities that nurture your shared sense of purpose.

Building Trust:

- Trust is the foundation of intimacy. Be reliable, keep your promises, and demonstrate loyalty to strengthen the bond of trust.

- Address and resolve any trust issues that may be hindering intimacy.

Shared Dreams and Goals:

- Intimacy flourishes when both partners are moving toward common goals. Discuss and align your aspirations to create a united vision for the future.

- Support each other's individual dreams, fostering a sense of teamwork.

Unconditional Acceptance:

- Embrace each other for who you are, flaws and all. Acceptance creates a sense of security and allows for genuine connection.

- Celebrate your differences and appreciate the unique qualities that make your relationship special.

Spontaneity and Playfulness:

- Infuse spontaneity and playfulness into your relationship. Break from routine, try new activities, and keep the element of surprise alive.

- Laughter and joy are powerful tools in strengthening the emotional connection.

Understanding the dynamics of intimacy involves a holistic approach that considers the emotional, intellectual, physical, and spiritual facets of your relationship. By nurturing each aspect, husbands can create a profound and lasting connection with their spouses, reigniting the passion that initially brought them together.

The various factors that contribute to a decline in intimacy

A decline in intimacy within a marriage can be attributed to various factors, and recognizing these challenges is the first step toward addressing and overcoming them. Here are several common factors that contribute to a decline in intimacy:

Communication Breakdown:

- Poor communication or a lack of effective communication can lead to misunderstandings and emotional distance.

- Unresolved conflicts and unexpressed feelings may build up over time, creating a barrier between partners.

Stress and Busy Lifestyles:

- High levels of stress, whether from work, financial pressures, or other life demands, can take a toll on emotional and physical intimacy.

- Busy schedules may result in couples spending less quality time together, diminishing opportunities for connection.

Unresolved Conflicts:

- Lingering conflicts that are not addressed can erode trust and emotional closeness.

- The avoidance of difficult conversations may lead to a sense of distance between partners.

Lack of Quality Time:

- Spending insufficient quality time together can contribute to a decline in intimacy.

- Neglecting shared activities and experiences can lead to a sense of emotional detachment.

Changes in Physical Intimacy

- Changes in sexual frequency or satisfaction can impact overall intimacy.

- Physical health issues, hormonal changes, or unmet sexual needs can contribute to a decline in physical closeness.

External Influences:

- External factors such as family issues, societal pressures, or interference from third parties can strain a relationship.

- Lack of boundaries with friends or family members may contribute to relationship stress.

Lack of Emotional Support:

- Failure to provide emotional support during challenging times can create a sense of isolation.

- Feeling emotionally unsupported may lead to a breakdown in the overall connection between partners.

Loss of Connection:

- Over time, couples may experience a loss of the initial spark and connection that brought them together.

- Neglecting the emotional and romantic aspects of the relationship can contribute to this sense of loss.

Unmet Expectations:

- Unrealistic expectations or unmet needs within the relationship can lead to disappointment and dissatisfaction.

- Communicating and aligning expectations is crucial to maintaining a healthy connection.

Negative Life Events:

- Traumatic events, such as the loss of a loved one, financial crises, or health issues, can impact emotional well-being and strain a relationship.

- Coping with these events together is essential for maintaining intimacy.

Recognizing these factors allows couples to proactively address issues and work towards rebuilding intimacy. Open communication, a willingness to invest time and effort, and a commitment to understanding and supporting each other are key elements in overcoming challenges and fostering a strong, intimate connection.

The impact of stress, communication issues, and lifestyle changes on a relationship

The impact of stress, communication issues, and lifestyle changes on a relationship can be profound, affecting various aspects of the partnership. Understanding these dynamics is crucial for couples seeking to navigate challenges and strengthen their bond. Here's a closer look at how each factor can influence a relationship:

Stress:

- Emotional Distance: High levels of stress can lead to emotional distance between partners. The focus on individual stressors may result in less emotional availability for each other.

- Decreased Intimacy: Stress can contribute to a decline in physical intimacy as individuals may find it challenging to relax and connect on a deeper level.

- Conflict and Tension: Unmanaged stress may lead to increased conflict within the relationship, as individuals may be more prone to irritability and frustration.

Communication Issues:

- Misunderstandings: Poor communication often leads to misunderstandings, creating a breeding ground for conflict and resentment.

- Isolation: Ineffective communication can result in emotional isolation, where partners feel unheard or misunderstood.

- Lack of Emotional Connection: A breakdown in communication may hinder the development of emotional intimacy, as couples struggle to connect on a deeper level.

Lifestyle Changes:

- Shift in Priorities: Significant lifestyle changes, such as career shifts, relocation, or becoming parents, can shift priorities and impact the time and energy available for the relationship.

- Loss of Shared Time: Busy lifestyles may result in couples spending less quality time together, leading to a sense of emotional distance.

- Adaptation Challenges: Adjusting to new routines and responsibilities can create stress and tension if partners fail to adapt together.

Cumulative Effect:

- Compounding Impact: Stress, communication issues, and lifestyle changes often interact, creating a compounding effect. For example, increased stress may exacerbate communication challenges, leading to a further strain on the relationship.

- Cycles of Neglect: A lack of effective communication or coping mechanisms in response to lifestyle changes can create cycles of neglect, where partners feel increasingly distant over time.

Health Impact:

- Physical and Mental Well-being: Prolonged stress and unresolved communication issues can have adverse effects on both partners' physical and mental well-being.

- Decreased Relationship Satisfaction: The cumulative impact of these factors may contribute to a decline in overall relationship satisfaction.

Coping Mechanisms:

- Individual Coping Strategies: Individuals may develop coping mechanisms such as withdrawal, avoidance, or unhealthy behaviors to deal with stress or communication challenges, further complicating the relationship dynamics.

- Seeking External Support: In some cases, seeking external support, such as counseling or therapy, can provide couples with effective tools to navigate these challenges.

Understanding the interconnected nature of stress, communication issues, and lifestyle changes is essential for couples aiming to fortify their relationship. Proactive communication, shared problem-solving, and a commitment to supporting each other through life's challenges are vital elements in preserving and enhancing the connection between partners.

The importance of empathy and understanding

Empathy and understanding are foundational elements in building and maintaining healthy relationships, including romantic partnerships. Here's a closer look at why these qualities is crucial:

Enhanced Communication:

- Listening Skills: Empathy involves not just hearing but actively listening to your partner. Understanding their perspective helps you respond in a way that fosters open communication.

- Validation: Demonstrating understanding through empathy validates your partner's feelings and experiences, creating a safe space for expression.

Conflict Resolution:

- Reduced Misunderstandings: Empathy allows you to see situations from your partner's point of view, reducing the likelihood of misunderstandings.

- Collaborative Problem-Solving: Understanding your partner's needs and concerns enables collaborative problem-solving, leading to more effective conflict resolution.

Emotional Connection:

- Deepened Emotional Intimacy: Empathy fosters a deep emotional connection by allowing you to connect with your partner on a more profound level.

- Shared Emotional Experience: Understanding your partner's emotions creates a sense of shared experience, strengthening the emotional bond between you.

Support During Challenges:

- Providing Comfort: Empathy enables you to offer genuine comfort and support when your partner is facing challenges or going through difficult times.

- Demonstrating Presence: Understanding your partner's emotions and being present with them reinforces the idea that you are there for them, enhancing feelings of security.

Building Trust:

- Openness and Vulnerability: Empathy encourages openness and vulnerability, as partners feel more comfortable expressing their thoughts and feelings without fear of judgment.

- Strengthening Trust: When your partner feels understood, trust is strengthened, creating a solid foundation for the relationship.

Promoting Emotional Well-being:

- Reducing Stress: Feeling understood and supported contributes to reduced stress levels for both partners.

- Emotional Validation: Empathy provides emotional validation, which is essential for mental and emotional well-being.

Cultivating a Positive Environment:

- Positive Atmosphere: An empathetic and understanding approach contributes to a positive and supportive atmosphere within the relationship.

- Promoting Positivity: By understanding your partner's needs and feelings, you can contribute to a more positive and harmonious environment.

Fostering Growth:

- Personal Growth: Empathy supports personal growth by encouraging partners to understand and accept each other's evolving needs and aspirations.

- Relationship Evolution: As individuals grow and change, empathy helps the relationship evolve, adapting to new dynamics and challenges.

Resolving Resentment:

- Preventing Resentment: Empathy helps address underlying issues and prevents the buildup of resentment, allowing for a healthier and more resilient relationship.

- Forgiveness and Understanding: Understanding your partner's perspective fosters forgiveness and helps move past conflicts.

In summary, empathy and understanding create a strong foundation for a thriving relationship. These qualities foster effective communication, promote emotional connection, and contribute to a supportive and positive environment. Prioritizing empathy in your interactions with your partner enhances the overall well-being of the relationship and allows it to grow and adapt over time.

Chapter 2
OPEN AND HONEST COMMUNICATION

Open and honest communication is a cornerstone of healthy relationships, fostering trust, understanding, and a strong emotional connection. Here's why it's crucial and how to cultivate it:

Building Trust:

- Transparency: Open communication involves being transparent about your thoughts, feelings, and experiences. This transparency builds trust between partners.

- Consistency: Consistently sharing information and being honest creates a predictable and trustworthy environment within the relationship.

Understanding Each Other:

- Expressing Feelings: Open communication allows partners to express their emotions, needs, and desires. This expression fosters a deeper understanding of each other.

- Active Listening: Actively listening to your partner's perspective is equally important. It demonstrates that their thoughts and feelings are valued.

Conflict Resolution:

- Addressing Issues Promptly: Open communication enables couples to address issues promptly rather than letting them fester. This proactive approach contributes to effective conflict resolution.

- Constructive Dialogue: Honest communication promotes constructive dialogue, where both partners can express their concerns and work together to find solutions.

Strengthening Intimacy:

- Vulnerability: Sharing your thoughts and feelings openly makes you vulnerable, creating a deeper emotional connection between partners.

- Intimate Conversations: Discussing intimate aspects of your relationship, such as desires and fears, fosters emotional intimacy.

Establishing Boundaries:

- Setting Expectations: Open communication helps in setting clear expectations and boundaries within the relationship.

- Respecting Limits: Partners can express their needs and limits, fostering mutual respect and understanding.

Promoting Growth

- Supporting Individual Growth: Open communication encourages partners to share their personal goals and aspirations, supporting each other's individual growth.

- Evolving Together: As individuals evolve, open communication allows the relationship to adapt and grow together.

Preventing Assumptions:

- Avoiding Misunderstandings: Communicating openly helps prevent misunderstandings and assumptions that can arise when partners are not on the same page.

- Clarifying Intentions: Partners can clarify their intentions and motivations, reducing the likelihood of misinterpretation.

Creating a Safe Space:

- Non-Judgmental Atmosphere: Open communication establishes a non-judgmental atmosphere where partners feel safe expressing themselves without fear of criticism.

- Encouraging Honesty: Encouraging honesty, even about difficult topics, contributes to a supportive and understanding relationship.

Sharing Responsibilities:

- Division of Responsibilities: Openly discussing and agreeing upon responsibilities in the relationship promotes a sense of fairness and equality.

- Avoiding Resentment: Open communication helps prevent resentment from building up due to unmet expectations.

Cultivating a Healthy Relationship Culture:

- Modeling Behavior: By practicing open and honest communication, couples model a healthy relationship culture that positively influences other aspects of their lives.

- Creating a Foundation: Open communication creates a solid foundation for other relationship-building activities, such as problem-solving and shared decision-making.

Open and honest communication is a powerful tool for building and maintaining a healthy relationship. It establishes trust, deepens understanding, and creates an environment where both partners feel valued and heard. Regularly practicing open communication contributes to the long-term success and resilience of the relationship.

Guidance on fostering open communication with your spouse.

Fostering open communication with your spouse is essential for building a strong and healthy relationship. Here are some guidance and tips to help you cultivate open communication:

Create a Safe and Judgment-Free Space:

- Ensure that your conversations are conducted in an atmosphere where both partners feel safe expressing their thoughts and feelings without fear of judgment.

- Emphasize that honesty is valued and that the goal is to understand each other, not to criticize.

Active Listening:

- Practice active listening by giving your full attention to your spouse when they speak.

- Avoid interrupting, and instead, let your partner express themselves fully before responding.

Express Yourself Clearly:

- Clearly articulate your thoughts and feelings. Use "I" statements to express your emotions without blaming or accusing your partner.

- Be specific and provide examples to help your spouse understand your perspective.

Choose the Right Time and Place:

- Pick an appropriate time and place for important discussions. Avoid bringing up sensitive topics in the midst of other stressors or when emotions are high.

- Create a calm and comfortable environment conducive to open conversation.

Be Mindful of Non-Verbal Communication:

- Pay attention to non-verbal cues such as body language and facial expressions. These can convey emotions that might not be explicitly expressed verbally.

- Be mindful of your own non-verbal cues to ensure they align with your intended message.

Encourage and Accept Feedback:

- Welcome feedback from your spouse and be open to constructive criticism. This fosters a culture of mutual growth and understanding.

- Avoid becoming defensive and instead focus on understanding your partner's perspective.

Use "We" Language:

- Frame discussions using "we" language to convey a sense of unity and collaboration. This emphasizes that you are working together as a team.

- For example, say "How can we solve this?" instead of "How can you fix this?"

Set Aside Regular Check-In Times:

- Schedule regular check-in times to discuss the state of your relationship, your individual goals, and any concerns or challenges.

- This helps prevent issues from building up and ensures that both partners have dedicated time for communication.

Practice Empathy:

- Put yourself in your partner's shoes and try to understand their perspective. This empathetic approach encourages open communication and strengthens emotional bonds.

- Acknowledge your partner's feelings and validate their experiences.

Use Technology Wisely:

- Utilize technology to stay connected, especially if you have busy schedules. Regular texts, messages, or even short phone calls can help maintain a sense of connection.

- However, for important or sensitive discussions, choose face-to-face or phone conversations over text to avoid misunderstandings.

Seek Professional Help if Needed:

- If communication challenges persist or if there are deep-rooted issues, consider seeking the help of a relationship counselor or therapist. Professional guidance can provide additional tools and insights.

Remember that open communication is an ongoing process that requires commitment and effort from both partners. By creating an environment of trust, actively listening, and practicing empathy, you can build a foundation for open communication that strengthens your relationship over time.

The significance of active listening and expressing emotions

Active listening and expressing emotions are integral components of effective communication in a relationship. Both practices contribute significantly to building understanding, fostering emotional connection, and resolving conflicts. Here's a closer look at the significance of active listening and expressing emotions:

Active Listening:

Understanding:

- Significance: Active listening involves fully concentrating, understanding, responding, and remembering what your partner communicates.

- Impact: It demonstrates a genuine interest in your partner's thoughts and feelings, fostering a deeper understanding of their perspective.

Validation:

- Significance: Active listening communicates validation and respect for your partner's experiences and emotions.

- Impact: Feeling heard and validated contributes to a sense of emotional security and strengthens the emotional connection between partners.

Conflict Resolution:

- Significance: Active listening is crucial during conflicts, as it helps de-escalate situations and promotes constructive dialogue.

- Impact: Partners are more likely to find common ground and reach resolutions when they feel their concerns have been genuinely heard and understood.

Building Trust:

- Significance: Active listening builds trust by creating an environment where partners feel comfortable sharing their thoughts and vulnerabilities.

- Impact: Trust is the foundation of a healthy relationship, and active listening helps reinforce this foundation.

Reducing Misunderstandings:

- Significance: Misunderstandings often arise from miscommunication. Active listening minimizes the chances of misinterpretation.

- Impact: Clear communication helps prevent unnecessary conflicts and ensures that both partners are on the same page.

Encouraging Openness:

- Significance: Active listening encourages partners to be more open and transparent in their communication.

- Impact: A culture of openness fosters a stronger connection and promotes a willingness to share thoughts and feelings.

Expressing Emotions:

Emotional Connection:

- Significance: Expressing emotions, whether positive or negative, is essential for building a strong emotional connection.

- Impact: Sharing emotions allows partners to connect on a deeper level, enhancing the overall intimacy of the relationship.

Vulnerability:

- Significance: Expressing emotions requires vulnerability and authenticity.

- Impact: When both partners feel safe expressing their true emotions, it creates an environment where trust and intimacy can flourish.

Conflict Resolution:

- Significance: Expressing emotions during conflicts helps uncover underlying issues and facilitates resolution.

- Impact: Addressing emotions head-on prevents bottling up feelings, reducing the likelihood of future conflicts.

Understanding Needs:

- Significance: Emotions often convey unmet needs or desires.

- Impact: By expressing emotions, partners can communicate their needs more clearly, enabling the other to respond and offer support.

Promoting Empathy:

- Significance: Expressing emotions encourages empathy from the other partner.

- Impact: When both partners express and understand each other's emotions, it strengthens the empathetic connection, deepening the bond between them.

Self-Awareness:

- Significance: Expressing emotions promotes self-awareness, as individuals must identify and understand their own feelings.

- Impact: Increased self-awareness contributes to personal growth and allows individuals to communicate their needs more effectively.

Active listening and expressing emotions are interwoven practices that play pivotal roles in creating a healthy and thriving relationship. By listening actively, partners demonstrate respect and understanding, while expressing emotions fosters emotional connection and promotes a culture of openness and vulnerability. Both practices contribute to effective communication, conflict resolution, and the overall well-being of the relationship.

Effective communication strategies for discussing sensitive topics.

Discussing sensitive topics in a relationship requires careful and thoughtful communication to ensure that both partners feel heard and understood. Here are some effective communication strategies for addressing sensitive topics:

1. Choose the Right Time and Setting:

- Timing Matters: Pick a time when both you and your partner are calm and have sufficient time to discuss the topic without feeling rushed.

- Choose a Comfortable Setting: Select a private and comfortable environment where you can talk openly without distractions.

2. Use "I" Statements:

- Express Your Feelings: Frame your thoughts using "I" statements to express your feelings and perspective without sounding accusatory.

- Example: Instead of saying, "You always do this," say, "I feel hurt when..."

3. Practice Active Listening:

- Give Full Attention: Ensure that you are actively listening to your partner without interrupting.

- Reflect Back: Repeat what your partner has said to confirm understanding and show that you are engaged in the conversation.

4. Stay Calm and Collected:

- Manage Your Emotions: Keep your emotions in check, and if you feel overwhelmed, take a break and return to the conversation later.

- Avoid Blame: Focus on the issue at hand rather than blaming your partner. Use neutral language to discuss your concerns.

5. Use Soft Start-Up:

- Begin Positively: Start the conversation with a positive or appreciative statement to set a more constructive tone.

- Example: "I really value our relationship, and there's something I'd like to discuss that's been on my mind."

6. Express Empathy:

- Acknowledge Your Partner's Feelings: Show empathy by acknowledging your partner's emotions and demonstrating that you understand their perspective.

- Example: "I can see that this is difficult for you, and I appreciate your willingness to talk about it."

7. Focus on Solutions:

- Collaborate: Approach the conversation as a collaborative effort to find solutions rather than placing blame.

- Problem-Solve Together: Discuss potential solutions to the issue at hand, emphasizing teamwork.

8. Be Open to Feedback:

- Encourage Openness: Let your partner know that you are open to their thoughts and feedback.

- Example: "I want to understand your perspective better. Can you share your thoughts on this?"

9. Take Breaks When Needed:

- Recognize Overload: If the conversation becomes too intense, agree to take a break and revisit the discussion when both parties are calmer.

- Establish a Signal: Establish a non-verbal signal or a code word that indicates when one of you needs a break.

10. Seek Common Ground:

- Identify Shared Goals: Find common ground by identifying shared goals or concerns.

- Example: "Our relationship is important to both of us. How can we work together to address this issue?"

11. Consider Professional Help:

- Counseling or Mediation: If the topic is particularly sensitive, consider seeking the help of a relationship counselor or mediator to facilitate the conversation.

12. Follow Up:

- Check-In Afterwards: After discussing the sensitive topic, check in with each other to ensure that both of you are processing the conversation well.

- Express Gratitude: Thank your partner for their willingness to engage in a challenging conversation.

Remember that effective communication is an ongoing process, and it may take time to address and resolve sensitive topics. Patience, understanding, and a commitment to working together are key elements in successfully navigating these conversations.

Chapter 3
BUILDING EMOTIONAL CONNECTION

Building emotional connections is crucial for creating a strong and resilient relationship. Emotional connection forms the foundation for intimacy, trust, and overall relationship satisfaction. Here are strategies to help you build and strengthen emotional connection with your partner:

1. Prioritize Quality Time:

- Spend intentional, quality time together without distractions.

- Engage in activities that you both enjoy and that foster shared experiences.

2. Effective Communication:

- Practice active listening to truly understand your partner's thoughts and feelings.

- Share your own thoughts and emotions openly, using "I" statements to express yourself without blaming.

3. Express Appreciation:

- Regularly express gratitude and appreciation for your partner's qualities, actions, and contributions.

- Acknowledge the small, everyday gestures that make a positive impact on your relationship.

4. Show Empathy:

- Put yourself in your partner's shoes and strive to understand their perspective.

- Validate your partner's feelings even if you may not agree with their point of view.

5. Create Rituals of Connection:

- Establish regular rituals, such as morning routines, bedtime rituals, or weekly date nights, which provide opportunities for connection.

- These rituals can be simple but meaningful, creating a sense of stability and closeness.

6. Share Dreams and Goals:

- Discuss your individual dreams, aspirations, and goals for the future.

- Identify common goals and work together to support each other's individual pursuits.

7. Celebrate Successes Together:

- Celebrate achievements, both big and small, as a team.

- Shared joy reinforces the idea that you are each other's greatest supporters.

8. Be Vulnerable:

- Share your vulnerabilities and insecurities with your partner.

- Creating a space where you can be emotionally naked fosters a deeper connection.

9. Physical Affection:

- Incorporate physical touch into your daily interactions.

- Hug, kiss, hold hands, and engage in other forms of affection that convey love and closeness.

10. Surprise and Spontaneity:

- Infuse surprise and spontaneity into your relationship to keep things fresh.

- Plan unexpected gestures or activities to show your partner that you're thinking of them.

11. Forgive and Let Go:

- Practice forgiveness and let go of past grievances.

- Holding onto resentment can hinder emotional connection, so work together to heal and move forward.

12. Support During Challenges:

- Be a source of emotional support during challenging times.

- Demonstrate empathy, offer encouragement, and reassure your partner that you are there for them.

13. Cultivate Shared Interests:

- Develop and nurture shared hobbies or interests.

- Finding activities, you both enjoy can create a strong bond and provide opportunities for connection.

14. Maintain a Positive Ratio:

- Strive for a positive ratio of positive to negative interactions.

- Aim to have more positive moments, expressions of love, and affirmations than negative ones.

15. Counseling or Workshops:

- Consider relationship counseling or workshops that focus on building emotional connections.

- Professional guidance can provide valuable tools and insights.

Building emotional connections is an ongoing process that requires mutual effort and commitment. By consistently implementing these strategies, you can create a relationship rich in emotional intimacy and connection.

Ways to strengthen emotional bonds within the relationship.

Strengthening emotional bonds within a relationship is a dynamic and ongoing process that involves intentional efforts from both partners. Here are various ways to enhance and deepen emotional connections:

1. Effective Communication:

- Practice active listening to understand your partner's thoughts and feelings.

- Communicate openly and honestly, expressing your own emotions and thoughts.

2. Quality Time:

- Prioritize quality time together without distractions.

- Engage in activities that you both enjoy and that foster connection.

3. Express Appreciation:

- Regularly express gratitude for your partner's actions, qualities, and contributions.

- Acknowledge and celebrate each other's strengths and positive qualities.

4. Physical Affection:

- Incorporate physical touch into your daily routine, such as hugs, kisses, and cuddling.

- Physical affection releases oxytocin, known as the "love hormone," promoting bonding.

5. Shared Rituals:

- Establish shared rituals or routines, such as morning coffee together or a weekly movie night.

- These rituals create a sense of predictability and closeness.

6. Vulnerability and Trust:

- Share your vulnerabilities and insecurities with your partner.

- Build trust by being reliable, keeping promises, and demonstrating consistency.

7. Celebrate Milestones:

- Acknowledge and celebrate important milestones, both as individuals and as a couple.

- Reflecting on achievements fosters a sense of shared accomplishment.

8. Create a Supportive Environment:

- Provide emotional support during challenging times.

- Create a safe space where both partners feel comfortable expressing themselves without judgment.

9. Surprises and Spontaneity:

- Plan surprise gestures or spontaneous activities to keep the relationship exciting.

- Unexpected surprises can reignite the sense of adventure and joy.

The role of shared activities, quality time, and expressing appreciation

Shared activities, quality time, and expressing appreciation play vital roles in building and sustaining a healthy and fulfilling relationship. These elements contribute to the overall well-being of the partnership by fostering connection, intimacy, and a positive emotional climate. Here's a closer look at the role of each:

1. Shared Activities:

a. Building Shared Memories:

- Participating in activities together creates shared memories that contribute to the unique identity of the relationship.

- These shared experiences strengthen the bond between partners and provide a sense of connection.

b. Enhancing Communication:

- Engaging in shared activities provides a natural context for communication.

- Conversations that arise during these activities deepen understanding and strengthen emotional connection.

c. Promoting Teamwork:

- Collaborative activities require teamwork and cooperation, fostering a sense of partnership.

- Overcoming challenges together during shared activities builds a sense of unity and solidarity.

d. Reigniting Passion:

- Activities that bring joy or excitement can reignite passion and bring a sense of novelty to the relationship.

- Pursuing shared interests can be a source of ongoing excitement and fulfillment.

2. Quality Time:

a. Deepening Emotional Connection:

- Quality time involves focused, undivided attention, allowing partners to deepen their emotional connection.

- Being present in the moment and actively engaging with each other builds intimacy.

b. Nurture Communication:

- Quality time provides opportunities for open and meaningful communication.

- Conversations during quality time can involve sharing thoughts, feelings, and aspirations, reinforcing emotional intimacy.

c. Strengthening Trust:

- Spending quality time together builds a foundation of trust and emotional security.

- The reassurance of being a priority in each other's lives strengthens the bond between partners.

d. Creating Rituals:

- Establishing rituals during quality time, such as date nights or regular check-ins, fosters predictability and reinforces emotional connection.

- Rituals contribute to a sense of stability and commitment.

3. Expressing Appreciation:

a. Reinforcing Positivity:

- Expressing appreciation creates a positive atmosphere within the relationship.

- Acknowledging and highlighting each other's strengths and positive qualities contributes to a supportive environment.

b. Boosting Confidence:

- Regular expressions of appreciation boost each partner's confidence and self-esteem.

- Feeling valued and recognized strengthens the overall emotional well-being of individuals in the relationship.

c. Building Gratitude:

- Expressing appreciation encourages a culture of gratitude within the relationship.

- Gratitude enhances overall relationship satisfaction and reinforces positive behaviors.

d. Strengthening Emotional Bond:

- Vocalizing appreciation for both big and small gestures foster a sense of being seen and valued.

- It strengthens the emotional bond by reinforcing the idea that each partner's efforts are recognized and cherished.

shared activities, quality time, and expressing appreciation are integral components of a thriving relationship. These elements contribute to building a positive emotional climate, fostering intimacy, and reinforcing the connection between partners. Incorporating a balance of these aspects into your relationship can lead to greater satisfaction and resilience over time.

Practical exercises to enhance emotional intimacy.

Enhancing emotional intimacy involves intentional efforts to connect with your partner on a deeper emotional level. Here are some practical exercises and activities that can help foster emotional intimacy in your relationship:

1. Emotional Check-Ins:

- Set aside dedicated time for regular emotional check-ins.

- Ask open-ended questions like "How are you feeling today?" and actively listen to your partner's responses.

2. Shared Journaling:

- Maintain a shared journal where both partners can write down their thoughts, feelings, and experiences.

- Exchange journals periodically to gain insights into each other's perspectives.

3. Gratitude Sharing:

- Take turns expressing gratitude for specific actions or qualities in each other.

- This exercise promotes a positive focus and reinforces appreciation.

4. Five-Minute Daily Sharing:

- Spend five minutes each day sharing your highs, lows, and anything else on your mind.

- This quick check-in helps maintain ongoing communication and connection.

5. Memory Sharing:

- Share and reminisce about significant memories from your relationship.

- Discussing shared experiences strengthens the emotional bond.

6. Love Maps:

- Take inspiration from psychologist John Gottman's concept of "Love Maps."

- Ask each other questions to understand each other's dreams, fears, and life aspirations on a deeper level.

7. Bucket List Creation:

- Create a joint bucket list of activities, experiences, and goals you both want to accomplish.

- This exercise fosters shared dreams and a sense of adventure.

8. Appreciation Letters:

- Write appreciation letters to each other, highlighting specific qualities, actions, or moments you cherish.

- Exchange letters and take the time to discuss them together.

9. Shared Hobbies:

- Explore and adopt a new hobby or activity together.

- Learning something new as a team strengthens your connection and provides shared experiences.

Remember that the key to these exercises is genuine engagement and a commitment to open communication. Tailor them to fit your relationship dynamics and enjoy the process of deepening your emotional intimacy over time.

Chapter 4
ADDRESSING PHYSICAL INTIMACY

Addressing physical intimacy in a relationship involves open communication, mutual respect, and a willingness to understand each other's needs and boundaries. Here are some considerations and strategies for addressing physical intimacy:

1. Open Communication:

- Express Your Feelings: Share your thoughts and feelings about physical intimacy openly with your partner.

- Active Listening: Encourage your partner to share their perspective, and actively listen to understand their needs and desires.

2. Establish Comfortable Communication Channels:

- Create a Safe Space: Ensure that conversations about physical intimacy take place in a safe and non-judgmental environment.

- Choose Appropriate Times: Pick a time when both you and your partner are relaxed and can focus on the conversation without distractions.

3. Understand Each Other's Needs:

- Discuss Expectations: Talk about your expectations and desires concerning physical intimacy. Ensure that you have a clear understanding of each other's needs.

- Be Respectful: Respect your partner's boundaries and communicate on your own. A healthy relationship requires mutual understanding and agreement.

4. Seek Professional Guidance if Needed:

- Consider Couples Counseling: If physical intimacy issues persist or become a source of tension, consider seeking the help of a relationship counselor or sex therapist.

- Professional Guidance: A professional can offer guidance and strategies to address specific concerns and improve physical intimacy.

5. Explore Together:

- Try New Things: Explore new activities or experiences together to enhance physical intimacy.

- Open-Mindedness: Be open-minded and willing to try things that you both find comfortable and enjoyable.

6. Prioritize Emotional Connection:

- Emotional Intimacy: Understand that physical intimacy is often closely tied to emotional intimacy.

- Build Emotional Connection: Work on building emotional closeness and connection, as it can positively impact your physical relationship.

7. Be Patient and Understanding:

- Understand Changes: Recognize that physical intimacy may evolve and change over time.

- Patience: Be patient with each other, especially during periods of stress or life changes.

8. Check-In Regularly:

- Scheduled Check-Ins: Set aside time for regular check-ins to discuss your physical relationship.

- Feedback: Provide constructive feedback about what you enjoy and what you might want to explore.

9. Prioritize Mutual Pleasure:

- Mutual Satisfaction: Focus on ensuring mutual pleasure and satisfaction.

- Communication during Intimacy: Talk openly about preferences and communicate during intimate moments to enhance the experience.

Remember that every relationship is unique, and there is no one-size-fits-all solution. The key is ongoing communication, understanding, and a shared commitment to fostering a healthy and satisfying physical relationship.

Common issues that may affect physical intimacy.

Physical intimacy in a relationship can be affected by various factors, and it's not uncommon for couples to face challenges in this area. Understanding these issues is crucial for addressing them effectively. Here are some common issues that may affect physical intimacy:

1. Communication Challenges:

- Lack of Open Communication: Difficulty expressing desires, concerns, or expectations can hinder physical intimacy.

- Misunderstandings: Poor communication may lead to misunderstandings about each other's needs and preferences.

2. Stress and Fatigue:

- Work and Life Stress: High levels of stress from work, family, or other life events can impact sexual desire.

- Fatigue: Feeling constantly tired or overwhelmed can decrease energy and motivation for physical intimacy.

3. Relationship Conflict:

- Unresolved Issues: Lingering conflicts or unresolved issues in the relationship can create emotional distance.

- Emotional Disconnection: Emotional disconnection often translates into reduced physical intimacy.

4. Body Image and Self-Esteem:

- Body Insecurities: Concerns about one's physical appearance or body image can affect confidence.

- Low Self-Esteem: Low self-esteem may contribute to feeling undeserving of physical affection.

5. Lack of Emotional Connection:

- Emotional Distance: A lack of emotional connection can lead to a decline in physical intimacy.

- Prioritizing Emotional Bond: Strengthening emotional intimacy is often crucial for a satisfying physical relationship.

6. Medical or Hormonal Issues:

- Medical Conditions: Physical health issues or chronic conditions can impact sexual function.

- Hormonal Imbalances: Changes in hormonal levels, such as during pregnancy or menopause, can affect libido.

7. Performance Anxiety:

- Pressure to Perform: Anxiety about sexual performance or fear of disappointing a partner can be a barrier to intimacy.

- Overthinking: Overthinking or self-imposed pressure can hinder the natural flow of intimacy.

8. Past Trauma or Abuse:

- Unresolved Trauma: Past experiences of trauma or abuse can create emotional barriers to intimacy.

- Trust Issues: Rebuilding trust and creating a safe space is essential for overcoming trauma-related intimacy challenges.

9. Lack of Time and Prioritization:

- Busy Schedules: Busy lifestyles can lead to neglect of physical intimacy.

- Prioritization: Making time for each other and prioritizing intimacy is essential for maintaining a connection.

Addressing these issues often involves a combination of open communication, empathy, seeking professional help if needed, and a mutual commitment to understanding and meeting each other's needs. Couples should approach these challenges as opportunities for growth and connection rather than as insurmountable obstacles.

Tips for reigniting passion and exploring new aspects of intimacy.

Reigniting passion and exploring new aspects of intimacy in a relationship requires creativity, open communication, and a willingness to prioritize and invest in your connection. Here are some tips to help you reignite passion and explore new dimensions of intimacy:

1. Communicate Openly:

- Foster an environment where you both feel comfortable discussing your desires, fantasies, and boundaries.

- Be open about your own feelings and encourage your partner to express themselves without judgment.

2. Prioritize Quality Time:

- Set aside dedicated time for each other without distractions.

- Plan date nights or weekend getaways to focus on reconnecting and enjoying each other's company.

3. Experiment with Sensory Experiences:

- Explore sensory experiences, such as using scented candles, oils, or textures during intimate moments.

- Engage in activities that heighten sensory awareness, deepening the connection.

4. Introduce Variety:

- Change routines and introduce variety into your relationship, both in and out of the bedroom.

- Try new activities together to bring a sense of novelty and excitement.

5. Read and Learn Together:

- Explore literature or attend workshops about sexuality and intimacy together.

- Learning together can lead to new ideas and perspectives that you can incorporate into your relationship.

6. Share Fantasies:

- Share your fantasies and encourage your partner to do the same.

- Find ways to incorporate elements of each other's fantasies into your intimate moments.

7. Engage in Playful Activities:

- Participate in playful activities that bring out your inner child.

- Playfulness can enhance bonding and create a lighthearted atmosphere.

8. Incorporate Surprise and Spontaneity:

- Plan surprise gestures or spontaneous acts of affection.

- Unpredictability can add an element of excitement to your relationship.

9. Focus on Emotional Connection:

- Strengthen emotional intimacy, as it often lays the foundation for a passionate physical connection.

- Deep conversations and shared vulnerability contribute to emotional closeness.

Remember that the key to reigniting passion is a combination of intention, creativity, and open communication. Be attuned to each other's needs, stay curious, and be proactive in exploring new dimensions of intimacy together.

Couples communicate openly about their desires and boundaries.

Open communication about desires and boundaries is crucial for building a healthy and fulfilling relationship. Here are some tips for couples to communicate openly about these important aspects:

1. Create a Safe Space:

- Foster an environment where both partners feel safe expressing their thoughts and feelings without fear of judgment.

- Establish trust as the foundation for open communication.

2. Set Aside Dedicated Time:

- Designate specific times to discuss desires and boundaries, ensuring that you have each other's undivided attention.

- Avoid important discussions during times of stress or when either partner is preoccupied.

3. Use "I" Statements:

- Frame statements using "I" rather than "you" to express personal feelings and needs.

- For example, say "I would like..." instead of "You never..."

4. Active Listening:

- Practice active listening by fully concentrating on what your partner is saying without interruption.

- Paraphrase and repeat back what you've heard to ensure understanding.

5. Express Positive Affirmations:

- Acknowledge and appreciate your partner's efforts in expressing desires and boundaries.

- Positive affirmations create a supportive atmosphere.

6. Be Specific and Concrete:

- Clearly articulate your desires and boundaries with specific examples.

- Avoid vague statements and provide details to help your partner understand your perspective.

7. Encourage Mutual Sharing:

- Encourage your partner to express their desires and boundaries as well.

- Create an equal opportunity for both partners to contribute to the conversation.

8. Discuss Timing and Frequency:

- Discuss the timing and frequency of certain activities or expressions of intimacy.

- Understanding each other's preferences regarding timing can prevent misunderstandings.

9. Regular Check-Ins:

- Schedule regular check-ins to discuss any changes or updates to desires and boundaries.

- Relationships evolve, and ongoing communication is essential.

By incorporating these tips, couples can establish a foundation of open communication that allows them to navigate desires and boundaries with understanding, empathy, and mutual respect. Open communication contributes significantly to the overall health and longevity of a relationship.

Chapter 5
UNDERSTANDING FEMALE SEXUALITY

Understanding female sexuality is a complex and nuanced topic that involves considering physical, emotional, and psychological factors. Here are some key aspects to consider when exploring female sexuality:

1. Diversity of Experience:

- Individual Differences: Female sexuality is highly individual, and there is no one-size-fits-all experience.

- Diverse Desires: Women may have diverse sexual desires, preferences, and needs.

2. Emotional Connection:

- Emotional Intimacy: Many women emphasize the importance of emotional connection for a fulfilling sexual experience.

- Communication: Open communication about feelings, desires, and boundaries is crucial.

3. Variety in Desires:

- Different Desires at Different Times: A woman's desires can vary throughout her life and may be influenced by factors like age, relationship status, and health.

- Exploration: Women may explore different aspects of their sexuality to understand their preferences.

4. Understanding Anatomy:

- Clitoral Stimulation: The clitoris is a key area for sexual pleasure in many women, and understanding its anatomy is essential.

- Vaginal Health: Understanding vaginal health, including the importance of arousal and lubrication, contributes to a positive sexual experience.

5. Mind-Body Connection:

- Psychological Factors: The mind-body connection plays a significant role in female sexuality.

- Stress and Anxiety: High levels of stress or anxiety can impact sexual desire and satisfaction.

6. Communication About Pleasure:

- Expressing Desires: Encouraging women to communicate openly about their desires and preferences is crucial.

- Mutual Exploration: Partners should engage in mutual exploration to discover what brings pleasure to both individuals.

7. Sexual Response Cycle:

- Desire, Arousal, Orgasm: Understanding the sexual response cycle, including phases of desire, arousal, and orgasm, can provide insights into female sexuality.

- Variability: The cycle can vary among individuals and across different circumstances.

8. Importance of Consent:

- Consent: Consent is fundamental in any sexual interaction. Ensuring that all parties are comfortable and willing is crucial for a healthy sexual relationship.

- Clear Communication: Openly communicating boundaries and obtaining explicit consent fosters a respectful and consensual environment.

9. Sexual Education:

- Comprehensive Sex Education: Adequate sexual education, including information about female anatomy, reproductive health, and pleasure, is essential.

- Ongoing Learning: Continuous learning about sexual health contributes to a positive sexual experience.

Understanding female sexuality requires ongoing education, open-mindedness, and a commitment to creating an environment that values communication, consent, and mutual satisfaction. By acknowledging the diversity of experiences and promoting a sex-positive and respectful culture, individuals and couples can navigate female sexuality with greater awareness and sensitivity.

Educate husbands on the nuances of female sexuality.

Understanding and respecting female sexuality is crucial for building strong and fulfilling relationships. Here are some nuanced insights for husbands:

Diverse Desires:

- Recognize that women, like men, have diverse sexual desires. What arouses or pleases one woman may differ from another. It's important to approach each other as unique individuals.

Emotional Connection Matters:

- For many women, emotional connection is closely tied to sexual satisfaction. Building trust, intimacy, and a sense of emotional security can greatly enhance the overall sexual experience.

Communication is Essential:

- Encourage open and honest communication about desires, preferences, and concerns. Create an environment where your wife feels comfortable expressing herself without fear of judgment.

Foreplay is Key:

- Understand that women often require more time for arousal. Prioritize extended periods of foreplay, including emotional connection, sensual touch, and verbal expressions of desire.

Explore Together:

- Be open to exploring new sexual experiences together. This could involve trying new activities, fantasies, or experimenting with different forms of intimacy. Mutual exploration fosters a deeper connection.

Understanding Anatomy:

- Familiarize yourself with female anatomy. Knowing the intricacies of her body and erogenous zones can enhance pleasure and contribute to a more satisfying sexual experience.

Quality Over Quantity:

- Recognize that the quality of intimacy is often more important than the quantity. Focus on creating meaningful, enjoyable, and connected moments rather than solely aiming for frequency.

Balance Initiatives:

- Share the responsibility of initiating sexual activity. This promotes a sense of equality and ensures that both partners feel desired and appreciated.

Respect Boundaries:

- Be attentive to your wife's boundaries and always prioritize consent. Respect her pace and comfort level and communicate openly about what feels right for both of you.

Educate Yourself Continuously:

- Stay informed about female sexuality. Read books, articles, or attend workshops that provide insights into women's sexual health. This ongoing education can strengthen your understanding and responsiveness.

Be Patient and Supportive:

- Female sexuality can be influenced by various factors, including hormonal changes, stress, and life events. Be patient, supportive, and understanding during times of fluctuation or change.

Remember, the key is to approach female sexuality with empathy, curiosity, and a commitment to mutual pleasure. Every woman is unique, so being attuned to your partner's needs and preferences is essential for fostering a satisfying and enduring intimate connection.

Insights into the emotional and physical aspects of a woman's sex drive

The sex drive, also known as libido, is a complex interplay of emotional, psychological, and physical factors. While individual experiences may vary, here are insights into the emotional and physical aspects of a woman's sex drive:

Emotional Aspects:

Relationship Quality:

- Emotional connection and intimacy with a partner often play a crucial role in a woman's sex drive.

- Feelings of love, trust, and security contribute positively to the emotional aspect of sexuality.

Stress and Mental Health:

- Stress, anxiety, and depression can negatively impact libido. High-stress levels may lead to a decrease in sexual desire.

- Mental health issues and unresolved emotional conflicts can also influence a woman's interest in sexual activity.

Body Image and Confidence:

- Positive body image and self-esteem are linked to higher levels of sexual satisfaction.

- Societal expectations and cultural factors can influence a woman's perception of her own body and impact her confidence in the bedroom.

Communication:

- Open and honest communication with a partner is essential. Discussing desires, preferences, and any concerns fosters a healthy sexual relationship.

Life Changes and Transitions:

- Major life events such as pregnancy, childbirth, menopause, or changes in relationship status can influence a woman's sex drive.

Physical Aspects:

Hormonal Fluctuations:

- Hormones, such as estrogen and progesterone, play a key role in regulating a woman's sex drive. Hormonal changes during the menstrual cycle, pregnancy, and menopause can affect libido.

Physical Health:

- Overall health, including cardiovascular health, can impact sexual function. Regular exercise and a balanced diet contribute to general well-being, potentially positively influencing libido.

Medications

- Certain medications, including contraceptives, antidepressants, and antihypertensives, may have side effects that influence sexual desire.

Physical Comfort and Wellness:

- Physical comfort, including absence of pain or discomfort during intercourse, is crucial for a positive sexual experience.

- Fatigue or lack of energy can also affect a woman's interest in sex.

Neurotransmitters:

- Neurotransmitters like dopamine and serotonin play a role in sexual arousal and satisfaction. Imbalances can impact mood and desire.

Intersection of Emotional and Physical Aspects:

Cultural and Social Factors:

- Cultural attitudes towards sexuality and societal expectations can influence both the emotional and physical aspects of a woman's sex drive.

Communication and Intimacy:

- Emotional intimacy, trust, and effective communication contribute to a positive sexual experience. Conversely, relationship issues can lead to a decrease in libido.

Fantasy and Desire:

- Emotional and psychological factors often intertwine with fantasies and desires, contributing to sexual arousal.

It's important to note that individual experiences vary, and a woman's sex drive is influenced by a combination of these factors. Open communication, a supportive environment, and a focus on overall well-being are key elements in maintaining a healthy and satisfying sexual relationship. If concerns about libido persist, consulting with a healthcare professional or a qualified sex therapist may be beneficial.

Practical advice on how to support and understand your spouse's needs.

Supporting and understanding your spouse's needs is crucial for a healthy and thriving relationship. Here are some practical pieces of advice to help you achieve that:

Effective Communication:

- Active Listening: Pay attention when your spouse is talking. Show that you're engaged by making eye contact, nodding, and responding appropriately.

- Open Dialogue: Encourage your spouse to express their thoughts and feelings openly. Create a safe space for them to share without judgment.

Empathy:

- Put Yourself in Their Shoes: Try to understand your spouse's perspective. Consider their emotions and experiences before reacting to a situation.

- Validate Their Feelings: Acknowledge your spouse's emotions, even if you don't necessarily agree with them. Validation fosters a sense of understanding.

Quality Time:

- Be Present: Spend quality time together without distractions. Put away electronic devices and focus on each other.

- Shared Activities: Find activities you both enjoy and can do together. This strengthens your bond and creates shared experiences.

Learn Their Love Language:

- Discover Each Other's Love Language: Take the time to understand how your spouse expresses and receives love. This can be through acts of service, words of affirmation, physical touch, quality time, or gifts.

Provide Emotional Support:

- Ask and Listen: Inquire about your spouse's day, concerns, or joys. Let them know you're there to support them emotionally.

- Offer Encouragement: Be a source of encouragement during challenging times. Remind your spouse of their strengths and capabilities.

Respect Boundaries:

- Understand Personal Space: Respect your spouse's need for alone time or personal space. Everyone requires moments of solitude.

- Discuss Boundaries: Communicate openly about boundaries in your relationship. Understand each other's comfort levels and expectations.

Share Responsibilities:

- Collaborate on Household Tasks: Divide responsibilities based on each other's strengths and preferences. This helps in creating a balanced partnership.

- Support Each Other's Goals: Encourage and support your spouse in pursuing their personal and professional goals.

Express Appreciation:

- Show Gratitude: Regularly express appreciation for the things your spouse does for you and the relationship.

- Complement Each Other: Compliments and positive affirmations strengthen the emotional connection.

Handle Conflicts Constructively:

- Stay Calm: When conflicts arise, remain calm and avoid escalating the situation.

- Use "I" Statements: Express your feelings using "I" statements to avoid blame and foster understanding.

Continuous Growth:

- Grow Together: Support each other's personal growth and development. Be open to learning and evolving as individuals and as a couple.

- Seek Professional Help: If needed, don't hesitate to seek the assistance of a couples' therapist or counselor to navigate challenges together.

Remember, the key is to be attentive, respectful, and proactive in meeting each other's needs. Regular communication and a willingness to invest time and effort in your relationship contribute to a strong and supportive connection.

Chapter 6

LIFESTYLE CHANGES FOR ENHANCED INTIMACY

Enhancing intimacy often involves a combination of emotional, physical, and relational factors. Here are some lifestyle changes and considerations that can contribute to improved intimacy:

Communication:

- Open Communication: Foster open and honest communication with your partner. Discuss your desires, needs, and boundaries to ensure both of you are on the same page.

- Active Listening: Practice active listening to understand your partner's feelings, concerns, and desires. This can strengthen your emotional connection.

Quality Time:

- Prioritize Time Together: Make an effort to spend quality time with your partner. This could involve date nights, weekend getaways, or even just quiet evenings at home without distractions.

Physical Health:

- Regular Exercise: Exercise is not only good for physical health but also for boosting mood and confidence, which can positively impact intimacy.

- Healthy Diet: A nutritious diet can contribute to overall well-being, including energy levels and physical health.

Mental Health:

- Stress Management: Find healthy ways to manage stress, such as mindfulness, meditation, or hobbies. High stress levels can negatively affect intimacy.

- Therapy or Counseling: Seeking therapy individually or as a couple can be beneficial for addressing underlying issues and improving communication.

Self-Care:

- Prioritize Self-Care: Take care of yourself physically and emotionally. When you feel good about yourself, it can positively impact your confidence and how you relate to your partner.

Intimacy Building Activities:

- Shared Hobbies: Engage in activities you both enjoy, whether it's a sport, art, or any other shared interest. This can strengthen your connection.

- Surprises and Spontaneity: Adding an element of surprise or spontaneity can keep the relationship exciting.

Technology and social media:

- Digital Detox: Consider taking breaks from technology to focus on each other without distractions.

- Mindful Social Media Use: Be mindful of the impact of social media on your relationship. Set boundaries and prioritize real-life interactions.

Adventure and Exploration:

- Try New Things Together: Whether it's trying a new hobby, exploring a new place, or even trying new things in the bedroom, novelty can bring excitement to a relationship.

Understanding Love Languages:

- Identify Love Languages: Learn about your partner's love language and communicate your own. Understanding how each of you expresses and receives love can deepen emotional connection.

Setting Boundaries:

- Respect Boundaries: Clearly communicate and respect each other's boundaries. This creates a safe and trusting environment.

Remember, the key is to be open, flexible, and willing to adapt to each other's needs. Every relationship is unique, so it's important to continuously communicate and make adjustments as needed.

The impact of lifestyle factors on intimacy

Lifestyle factors can have a significant impact on intimacy in a relationship. Intimacy encompasses emotional, physical, and sexual closeness between partners. Here are some lifestyle factors that can influence intimacy:

Communication Styles:

- Effective communication is crucial for maintaining emotional intimacy. A lack of communication or poor communication skills can lead to misunderstandings and distance between partners.

Work-Life Balance:

- Busy work schedules and excessive stress can affect the time and energy available for intimate moments. It's important for partners to find a balance that allows for quality time together.

Physical Health:

- Physical health plays a role in intimacy. Chronic illnesses, fatigue, or physical discomfort can impact one's ability to engage in physical and sexual activities, potentially affecting intimacy.

Mental Health:

- Mental health issues, such as anxiety or depression, can impact emotional intimacy. It's important for partners to support each other and seek professional help if needed.

Technology Use:

- Excessive use of technology, particularly smartphones and social media, can lead to distraction and reduced quality time spent together. Creating boundaries around technology can enhance intimacy.

Financial Stress:

- Financial difficulties can create tension and stress in a relationship, affecting emotional and sexual intimacy. Open communication about finances and collaborative financial planning can help mitigate this stress.

Cultural and Religious Beliefs:

- Differences in cultural or religious beliefs may influence views on intimacy. Understanding and respecting each other's perspectives can help navigate potential conflicts.

Prioritizing Quality Time:

- Intimacy requires time and effort. Partners need to prioritize spending quality time together, whether through shared activities, date nights, or simple moments of connection.

Parenting:

- Parenting responsibilities can be demanding, leaving little time for intimacy. It's essential for parents to find ways to connect and maintain their romantic relationship amidst the challenges of raising a family.

Self-Care:

- Individual self-care is crucial for maintaining a healthy relationship. When individuals take care of their physical and mental well-being, they are more likely to contribute positively to the intimacy of the relationship.

Understanding and addressing these lifestyle factors can contribute to a healthier and more intimate relationship. It's important for partners to communicate openly, support each other, and be proactive in maintaining and enhancing intimacy over time. Seeking professional help, such as couples therapy, can also be beneficial in addressing specific challenges.

Guidance on creating a conducive environment for intimacy.

Creating a conducive environment for intimacy involves both physical and emotional aspects. Here are some suggestions to help you set the stage for a more intimate atmosphere:

Communication:

- Open and honest communication is crucial. Discuss your desires, boundaries, and expectations with your partner to ensure you both feel comfortable and respected.

- Express your feelings and listen to your partner's needs as well. This builds emotional intimacy, making the physical connection more meaningful.

Comfortable Setting:

- Ensure the physical space is comfortable and inviting. This includes clean sheets, soft lighting, and a clutter-free environment.

- Consider incorporating elements that appeal to the senses, such as scented candles, soft music, or comfortable textures.

Privacy:

- Create a private space where you and your partner can feel secure and free from interruptions. This may involve setting boundaries with others in your living space or finding a private location.

Mood Lighting:

- Soft, dim lighting can help create a relaxed and intimate atmosphere. Consider using candles, fairy lights, or a dimmer switch to control the brightness.

Sensory Stimulation:

- Engage the senses to enhance the experience. This can include pleasant scents, soothing music, and even incorporating tactile elements like soft fabrics or massage oils.

Personal Touch:

- Personalize the space with items that have sentimental value or that remind you of shared experiences. This can help create a sense of connection and intimacy.

Mutual Consent and Respect:

- Ensure that both partners are comfortable and enthusiastic about the intimate experience. Consent and respect are fundamental to creating a safe and enjoyable environment.

Relaxation Techniques:

- Encourage relaxation through activities like deep breathing, meditation, or a warm bath. A relaxed mind and body contribute to a more intimate experience.

Romantic Gestures:

- Show affection through small gestures like holding hands, cuddling, or giving compliments. These expressions of love contribute to a warm and affectionate atmosphere.

Time and Presence:

- Take the time to be present with your partner. Put away distractions like phones and focus on each other. Building emotional connection fosters a more intimate environment.

Remember that every individual and relationship is unique, so it's important to be attuned to your partner's preferences and comfort levels. Regularly checking in and adapting your approach based on mutual communication can contribute to a continuously conducive environment for intimacy.

The role of health, exercise, and relaxation in improving overall well-being

Health, exercise, and relaxation play crucial roles in improving overall well-being, encompassing physical, mental, and emotional aspects. Here's an overview of each component:

Health:

- Physical Health: A healthy body is the foundation of overall well-being. Proper nutrition, sufficient hydration, and regular health check-ups contribute to physical well-being. Adequate sleep is also vital for physical health as it allows the body to repair and rejuvenate.

- Prevention of Diseases: Healthy lifestyle choices, such as maintaining a balanced diet, regular exercise, and avoiding harmful habits (like smoking and excessive alcohol consumption), can significantly reduce the risk of chronic diseases.

- Energy Levels: Good health is associated with higher energy levels, enabling individuals to engage in daily activities more effectively.

Exercise:

- Physical Fitness: Regular exercise has numerous benefits for physical health, including improved cardiovascular health, muscle strength, and flexibility. It also helps maintain a healthy weight.

- Mental Health: Exercise is linked to the release of endorphins, which are neurotransmitters that contribute to feelings of happiness and reduce stress. Physical activity has been shown to alleviate symptoms of depression and anxiety.

- Cognitive Function: Exercise has positive effects on cognitive function and can help prevent age-related decline in mental abilities. It enhances memory, attention, and overall brain health.

Relaxation:

- Stress Reduction: Chronic stress can negatively impact both physical and mental well-being. Relaxation techniques, such as deep breathing, meditation, and mindfulness, can help reduce stress levels.

- Emotional Well-being: Taking time for relaxation and leisure activities fosters emotional well-being. Engaging in hobbies, spending time with loved ones, or simply enjoying quiet moments contribute to a positive emotional state.

- Improved Sleep: Relaxation techniques can also aid in better sleep quality. Quality sleep is essential for overall health and well-being, as it supports physical recovery and mental clarity.

Health, exercise, and relaxation are interconnected elements that contribute synergistically to overall well-being. Incorporating a balanced approach to these components in daily life can lead to improved physical health, enhanced mental well-being, and a better overall quality of life. It's important to consult with healthcare professionals and fitness experts to tailor these practices to individual needs and conditions.

Chapter 7
SEEKING PROFESSIONAL HELP

If you're seeking professional help, that's a positive step towards addressing whatever challenges you may be facing. The type of professional you reach out to will depend on the nature of your concern. Here are some common areas and the corresponding professionals you might consider:

Mental Health:

- Psychologist or Counselor: For talk therapy and support.

- Psychiatrist: For medication management and therapy.

Medical Health:

- General Practitioner (GP): For general health concerns and referrals to specialists.

- Specialists: Depending on your specific health issue.

Financial Issues:

- Financial Planner: For general financial advice and planning.

- Debt Counselor: For managing and reducing debt.

Legal Matters:

- Lawyer: For legal advice and representation.

Career Guidance:

Career Counselor or Coach: For help with career choices and development.

Relationships:

- Couples Therapist or Marriage Counselor: For relationship issues.

- Family Therapist: For addressing family dynamics and conflicts.

Addiction Issues:

- Addiction Counselor or Therapist: Specializes in helping with substance abuse.

Life Coaching:

- Life Coach: For support and guidance in various life aspects.

If you're unsure where to start, consider reaching out to a general practitioner, who can provide guidance or refer you to the appropriate specialist. Additionally, many communities have helplines or crisis intervention services available.

Remember, seeking professional help is a proactive and positive step toward taking care of your well-being. If you're in crisis, don't hesitate to contact emergency services or a crisis hotline.

The importance of seeking professional advice when needed.

- Seeking professional advice is important in various aspects of life, and it plays a crucial role in personal, professional, and even financial well-being. Here are several reasons highlighting the importance of seeking professional advice when needed:

- Expertise and Knowledge: Professionals have specialized knowledge and expertise in their respective fields. Whether it's legal, medical, financial, or any other area, professionals have undergone extensive training and education to understand complex issues and provide accurate information.

- Avoiding Mistakes: Professionals can help you avoid common mistakes and pitfalls associated with a particular field. They can guide you through processes, alert you to potential risks, and offer insights based on their experience, reducing the likelihood of errors.

- Legal Compliance: In many situations, especially in legal matters or business transactions, it is crucial to comply with laws and regulations. Seeking professional advice ensures that you are aware of and adhere to the relevant legal requirements, avoiding legal complications.

- Saving Time and Resources: Professionals can streamline processes and help you make more informed decisions, ultimately saving you time and resources. Their expertise allows for efficient problem-solving and decision-making, reducing the need for trial and error.

- Customized Solutions: Professionals can provide personalized advice tailored to your specific situation. They take into account your individual circumstances, preferences, and goals to offer advice that is relevant and beneficial to you.

- Objective Perspective: Professionals can offer an objective viewpoint on your situation. They are not emotionally invested in your decisions and can provide unbiased advice, helping you see the bigger picture and make more rational choices.

- Continual Learning and Updates: Many fields undergo regular changes, whether it's tax laws, medical advancements, or technological updates. Professionals stay current with these changes and can provide advice based on the latest information, ensuring that you make decisions that align with current standards and practices.

- Peace of Mind: Knowing that you've sought advice from a qualified professional can provide peace of mind. Whether it's for health concerns, legal matters, or financial decisions, having confidence in your choices can reduce stress and anxiety.

- Long-Term Planning: Professionals can assist in long-term planning, helping you set and achieve your goals. Whether it's retirement planning, estate planning, or career development, their guidance can contribute to your overall success and well-being.

Seeking professional advice is a wise and proactive approach to navigating various aspects of life. It adds a layer of expertise, experience, and objectivity to your decision-making process, ultimately contributing to better outcomes and a more secure future.

Information on couples therapy and other resources

Couples therapy, also known as couples counseling or marriage therapy, is a type of psychotherapy that aims to help couples recognize and resolve conflicts, improve their communication, and enhance their relationship. Here is some information on couples therapy and additional resources:

**1. ** Goals of Couples Therapy:

- Communication Improvement: Enhancing communication skills to promote better understanding and empathy.

- Conflict Resolution: Identifying and resolving conflicts in a healthy and constructive manner.

- Intimacy Building: Fostering emotional and physical intimacy within the relationship.

- Problem-Solving: Developing effective problem-solving strategies as a couple.

**2. ** Common Issues Addressed:

- Communication problems

- Infidelity

- Financial conflicts

- Intimacy issues

- Parenting disagreements

- Substance abuse

- Cultural or religious differences

**3. ** Approaches to Couples Therapy:

- Cognitive-Behavioral Therapy (CBT): Focuses on changing negative patterns of thinking and behavior.

- Emotionally Focused Therapy (EFT): Concentrates on the emotional bonds between partners.

- Gottman Method: Developed by Drs. John and Julie Gottman, emphasizes building relationship skills and addressing conflicts.

**4. ** Finding a Couples Therapist:

- Ask for Recommendations: Seek recommendations from friends, family, or healthcare professionals.

- Online Directories: Use online directories to find licensed therapists in your area.

- Professional Organizations: Check organizations such as the American Association for Marriage and Family Therapy (AAMFT).

**5. ** Books on Couples Therapy:

- "The Seven Principles for Making Marriage Work" by John Gottman

- "Hold Me Tight" by Sue Johnson

- "Getting the Love, You Want" by Harville Hendrix

**6. ** Online Resources:

- Therapy Apps: Platforms like Better Help and Talk space offer online therapy services.

- Online Workshops: Some therapists conduct virtual workshops on relationship skills.

- Articles and Blogs: Websites like Psychology Today often have articles on relationship issues.

**7. ** Workshops and Seminars:

- Local Events: Look for workshops or seminars on relationships in your community.

- Relationship Retreats: Some organizations offer retreats focusing on couples' well-being.

**8. ** Community Support:

- Support Groups: Local or online support groups can provide a sense of community and shared experiences.

- Religious or Cultural Resources: Some couples find support through their religious or cultural communities.

**9. ** Self-Help Resources:

- Journaling: Reflecting on your thoughts and feelings can promote self-awareness.

- Relationship Workbooks: Workbooks designed for couples can guide self-help efforts.

Remember that seeking professional help is crucial for more serious or persistent relationship issues. A licensed therapist can provide tailored guidance based on your specific situation.

Importance of addressing a sexless marriage

Addressing a sexless marriage is crucial for various reasons, as it directly impacts the overall health and well-being of the relationship. Here are some key reasons why it's important to address and work on resolving issues related to a sexless marriage:

- Emotional Connection: Physical intimacy is a vital component of emotional connection between partners. It helps foster a sense of closeness, bonding, and trust. When a marriage lacks physical intimacy, the emotional connection can weaken over time.

- Quality of Life: A satisfying sexual relationship contributes to an overall sense of well-being and happiness. Couples who are physically intimate tend to experience higher levels of life satisfaction and report a better quality of life.

- Communication and Understanding: Addressing issues related to intimacy requires open and honest communication. By discussing the reasons behind a sexless marriage, couples can gain a better understanding of each other's needs, desires, and concerns.

- Prevention of Resentment: Lack of physical intimacy can lead to feelings of rejection, frustration, and resentment. Over time, these negative emotions can build up and strain the relationship, potentially leading to more serious problems.

- Physical Health Benefits: Sexual activity has physical health benefits, including stress reduction, improved immune function, and cardiovascular health. Maintaining a healthy sex life can positively impact both partners' physical well-being.

- Connection with the Past: Physical intimacy often plays a significant role in the initial stages of a romantic relationship. By addressing a sexless marriage, couples can reconnect with the positive experiences that brought them together in the first place.

- Enhanced Communication Skills: Working through issues related to intimacy requires effective communication skills. Addressing these challenges can improve a couple's ability to communicate and solve problems together.

- Rekindling Romance: Taking steps to address a sexless marriage can reignite the romantic spark between partners. Engaging in activities that promote intimacy can help revive feelings of attraction and passion.

- Long-Term Relationship Satisfaction: A healthy sexual relationship contributes to long-term relationship satisfaction. Couples who are physically connected are more likely to navigate challenges together and experience a fulfilling partnership.

- Overall Relationship Stability: A sexless marriage may contribute to relationship instability. By addressing and resolving intimacy issues, couples can build a stronger foundation for a stable and lasting partnership.

It's important for couples facing a sexless marriage to approach the issue with empathy, open communication, and a willingness to work together to find solutions that meet the needs of both partners. Seeking the assistance of a professional, such as a therapist or counselor, can also be beneficial in navigating these challenges.

Chapter 8

UNDERSTANDING THE PROBLEM

Understanding a problem is a crucial step in finding effective solutions. Whether you are dealing with a personal challenge, a work-related issue, or a broader societal problem, a systematic approach can help you gain clarity. Here's a general guide to understanding a problem:

Define the Problem:

- Clearly articulate what the problem is. Be specific and avoid vague descriptions.

- Identify the symptoms and root causes of the problem.

Gather Information:

- Collect relevant data and information related to the problem.

- Consider different perspectives and gather input from stakeholders.

Analyze the Situation:

- Break down the problem into smaller components to better understand its complexities.

- Identify patterns, trends, and relationships within the data.

Identify Stakeholders:

- Determine who is affected by the problem.

- Consider the interests, concerns, and perspectives of various stakeholders.

Understand Constraints:

- Recognize any limitations or constraints that may impact the problem-solving process.

- Consider factors such as time, budget, resources, and regulations.

Explore Solutions:

- Brainstorm potential solutions without judgment initially.

- Consider both short-term and long-term strategies.

Evaluate Options:

- Assess the feasibility, effectiveness, and potential risks of each solution.

- Prioritize solutions based on their impact and feasibility.

Make Decisions:

- Choose the best solution based on your analysis and evaluation.

- Consider the trade-offs and potential consequences of your decision.

Implement the Solution:

- Develop a plan for implementing the chosen solution.

- Allocate resources, assign responsibilities, and establish a timeline.

Monitor and Adjust:

- Regularly assess the progress of the implemented solution.

- Be willing to make adjustments or changes as needed.

Learn from the Process:

- Reflect on the problem-solving process.

- Identify lessons learned and apply them to future challenges.

Remember, effective problem-solving often involves collaboration and an open-minded approach. Be willing to adapt and iterate as you work towards a solution. Additionally, seeking input from others and considering diverse perspectives can lead to more comprehensive and innovative solutions.

Factors contributing to a sexless marriage.

A sexless marriage is typically defined as a relationship in which a couple has little to no sexual activity. Various factors can contribute to a sexless marriage, and it's essential to recognize that each couple's situation is unique. Some common factors include:

- Communication issues: Lack of open communication about sexual needs, desires, or concerns can lead to misunderstandings and a decline in intimacy.

- Stress and fatigue: High levels of stress, whether from work, financial pressures, or other life challenges, can contribute to a lack of energy and interest in sexual activities.

- Health issues: Physical and mental health problems, such as chronic illness, pain, depression, or anxiety, can affect libido and sexual function.

- Hormonal changes: Hormonal fluctuations, especially in women during pregnancy, postpartum, or menopause, can impact sexual desire.

- Relationship problems: Issues such as unresolved conflicts, trust issues, emotional distance, or a lack of emotional connection can negatively affect the overall intimacy within a relationship.

- Medication side effects: Some medications, such as certain antidepressants, antipsychotics, or hormonal contraceptives, may have side effects that include a decrease in libido.

- Life transitions: Major life changes like the birth of a child, children leaving home, or retirement can disrupt established routines and impact a couple's intimacy.

- Mismatched sexual needs: Differences in sexual preferences, desires, or frequency expectations can lead to dissatisfaction and avoidance of sexual activities.

- Cultural or religious factors: Societal or cultural influences, as well as religious beliefs, can impact a couple's views on sex and may contribute to a sexless marriage.

- Lack of time for intimacy: Busy schedules, work demands, and other commitments can leave little time for couples to prioritize and engage in intimate activities.

- Fear of rejection or performance anxiety: Individual concerns about one's appearance, sexual performance, or fear of rejection can lead to avoidance of sexual intimacy.

- Loss of attraction: Changes in physical appearance or emotional dynamics may contribute to a loss of attraction between partners.

It's important for couples facing these issues to communicate openly, seek professional help, if necessary (such as from a therapist or counselor), and work together to address the underlying causes of a sexless marriage. Identifying and addressing these factors can be crucial in rebuilding intimacy and strengthening the overall relationship.

Communication breakdown

"Communication breakdown" typically refers to a situation where there is a failure or disruption in the process of exchanging information between individuals or groups. This breakdown can occur for various reasons and at different levels, leading to misunderstandings, conflicts, and ineffective collaboration. Here are some common causes of communication breakdowns:

Lack of Clarity:

- Unclear or ambiguous messages can lead to misunderstandings. It's essential to express ideas and information in a clear and concise manner.

Poor Listening Skills:

- Ineffective listening can result in misinterpretation of information. It's important for all parties involved to actively listen and seek clarification when needed.

Assumptions:

- Making assumptions about what others know or understand can lead to communication breakdowns. It's crucial to confirm understanding and not rely solely on assumptions.

Noise:

- External factors, distractions, or interference can disrupt the communication process. This might include physical noise, technological issues, or even emotional distractions.

Cultural Differences:

- Varied cultural backgrounds may lead to different interpretations of messages. Awareness and sensitivity to cultural differences can help avoid misunderstandings.

Lack of Feedback:

- Without feedback, it's challenging to know if the message has been accurately received and understood. Encouraging open communication and providing opportunities for feedback can help.

Emotional Barriers:

- Emotional states of individuals can impact communication. Stress, frustration, or other strong emotions may hinder the ability to convey or receive messages effectively.

Hierarchy and Power Dynamics:

- Organizational hierarchies and power dynamics can create barriers to open communication. Subordinates may be hesitant to share information with superiors, fearing negative consequences.

Technology Issues:

- Problems with communication tools and technology can contribute to breakdowns. This includes issues with email, messaging apps, video conferencing, etc.

Different Communication Styles:

- Varied communication styles among team members can lead to misunderstandings. Some people may prefer written communication, while others may prefer verbal or visual communication.

To address communication breakdowns, it's crucial to promote effective communication strategies, foster a culture of open communication, and address any underlying issues that may be contributing to the breakdown. This might involve improving communication skills, providing training, and creating an environment where individuals feel comfortable expressing their thoughts and concerns.

Emotional disconnect.

"Emotional disconnect" typically refers to a state in which an individual feels a lack of emotional connection or resonance with their own feelings, others, or the world around them. It can manifest in various ways and may be temporary or chronic. Here are a few possible explanations and suggestions:

- Stress or Burnout: High levels of stress or burnout can lead to emotional exhaustion and detachment. In such cases, it's important to identify sources of stress and work on stress management techniques. This may involve setting boundaries, practicing self-care, and seeking support.

- Depression or Anxiety: Mental health conditions, such as depression or anxiety, can contribute to emotional disconnect. If you suspect a mental health issue, it's crucial to seek professional help. Therapy, counseling, or medication may be recommended based on the severity of the condition.

- Trauma: Past traumatic experiences can result in emotional numbness or dissociation as a coping mechanism. In these cases, therapy, particularly trauma-focused therapy, can be beneficial in processing and addressing the underlying issues.

- Relationship Issues: Strained relationships, whether with family, friends, or romantic partners, can lead to emotional disconnect. Communication is key in resolving conflicts and rebuilding emotional connections. Couples or family therapy may be helpful.

- Lifestyle Factors: Poor lifestyle habits, such as lack of sleep, unhealthy diet, or inadequate exercise, can impact emotional well-being. Ensuring a healthy lifestyle can contribute to improved emotional resilience.

- Existential Concerns: Sometimes, individuals experience an emotional disconnect due to existential questions or a lack of meaning in life. Exploring personal values, goals, and finding purpose can be part of a process to reconnect emotionally.

- Mindfulness and Self-awareness: Practices like mindfulness meditation can help individuals become more aware of their emotions and develop a greater connection with themselves. Mindfulness encourages being present in the moment and accepting emotions without judgment.

- Social Support: Building and maintaining strong social connections can provide emotional support and a sense of belonging. Engaging in activities with friends or participating in social groups can foster emotional connection.

If emotional disconnect persists or significantly impacts daily life, it's advisable to consult with a mental health professional. They can help identify the underlying causes and provide guidance on appropriate interventions for your specific situation.

Stress and external pressures

Stress is a physiological and psychological response to challenging situations or demands, often referred to as stressors. External pressures are factors from the environment that contribute to stress. Both can have significant effects on an individual's well-being and overall health. Here are some key points about stress and external pressures:

Stress:

- Definition: Stress is the body's natural response to a perceived threat or challenge. It triggers the "fight or flight" response, releasing stress hormones like cortisol and adrenaline.

Types of Stress:

- Acute Stress: Short-term stress triggered by specific events.

- Chronic Stress: Long-term stress, often resulting from ongoing situations or persistent issues.

Causes of Stress:

- Work-related: High workload, tight deadlines, job insecurity.

- Personal Relationships: Conflicts, breakups, family issues.

- Financial Pressure: Economic challenges, debt.

- Health Concerns: Chronic illnesses, injuries.

- Life Transitions: Moving, starting a new job, major life changes.

Effects of Stress:

- Physical Effects: Headaches, fatigue, muscle tension, digestive issues.

- Emotional Effects: Anxiety, irritability, depression.

- Behavioral Changes: Changes in eating or sleeping habits, social withdrawal.

Coping Strategies:

- Healthy Lifestyle: Regular exercise, balanced diet, sufficient sleep.

- Relaxation Techniques: Meditation, deep breathing, yoga.

- Time Management: Prioritizing tasks, setting realistic goals.

- Social Support: Talking to friends, family, or seeking professional help.

External Pressures:

- Definition: External pressures are factors in the environment that contribute to stress. They can be social, economic, or environmental.

Examples of External Pressures:

- Work Environment: Demanding job expectations, lack of resources.

- Social Expectations: Cultural norms, societal pressures.

- Economic Factors: Financial instability, job insecurity.

- Environmental Stressors: Pollution, noise, traffic.

Impact on Individuals:

- Professional Life: High work demands, competition, and job instability.

- Personal Life: Social expectations, family responsibilities.

- Economic Challenges: Financial difficulties, debt.

Mitigating External Pressures:

- Setting Boundaries: Establishing limits on work hours and commitments.

- Financial Planning: Budgeting and managing finances wisely.

- Social Support: Building a support network and seeking help when needed.

Organizational and Societal Changes:

- Flexible Work Policies: Supporting work-life balance.

- Social Policies: Addressing societal pressures and expectations.

Understanding and managing stress and external pressures involves a combination of personal strategies, social support, and, in some cases, broader societal changes. Developing resilience and coping mechanisms is crucial for maintaining well-being in the face of life's challenges.

Chapter 9
COMMUNICATION STRATEGIES

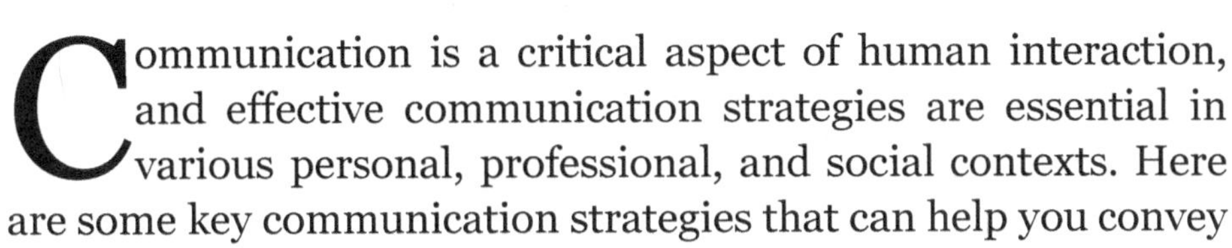

Communication is a critical aspect of human interaction, and effective communication strategies are essential in various personal, professional, and social contexts. Here are some key communication strategies that can help you convey your message more clearly and build stronger connections with others:

Active Listening:

- Give your full attention to the speaker.

- Avoid interrupting and allow the speaker to finish before responding.

- Use verbal and nonverbal cues to show that you are engaged, such as nodding and maintaining eye contact.

Clarity and Conciseness:

- Be clear and concise in your message to avoid misunderstandings.

- Use simple and straightforward language, especially when conveying complex ideas.

Nonverbal Communication:

- Pay attention to your body language, facial expressions, and gestures.

- Ensure that your nonverbal cues are consistent with your verbal message.

Empathy:

- Try to understand the other person's perspective and feelings.

- Acknowledge and validate their emotions to build rapport.

Adaptability:

- Be adaptable in your communication style based on the situation and the person you are communicating with.

- Recognize and respect cultural differences in communication.

Feedback:

- Seek and provide constructive feedback to improve understanding.

- Encourage open and honest communication by creating a feedback-friendly environment.

Open-Ended Questions:

- Use open-ended questions to encourage detailed responses and facilitate a deeper conversation.

- Avoid questions that can be answered with a simple "yes" or "no."

Use of Technology:

- Choose the appropriate communication channel for the context (e.g., email, phone, video conference).

- Use technology tools effectively to enhance communication.

Tone of Voice:

- Be mindful of your tone, as it can greatly influence how your message is received.

- Aim for a tone that is respectful, positive, and appropriate for the situation.

Conflict Resolution:

- Develop skills in resolving conflicts through effective communication.

- Focus on the issue at hand rather than making it personal.

Timing:

- Consider the timing of your communication, especially for sensitive or important matters.

- Choose the right moment to ensure receptiveness.

Visual Aids:

- Use visual aids when appropriate to enhance understanding.

- Visuals can be helpful in presentations, discussions, and educational contexts.

Remember that effective communication is a dynamic and ongoing process that requires practice and continuous improvement. Tailor your approach to the specific needs of the situation and the individuals involved.

Open and honest dialogue

Open and honest dialogue is a communication approach characterized by sincerity, transparency, and a genuine willingness to share thoughts, feelings, and information. In this type of dialogue, participants express their thoughts and emotions truthfully, without hidden agendas or manipulation. The aim is to foster mutual understanding, build trust, and create a foundation for effective communication.

Key principles of open and honest dialogue include:

- Transparency: Participants share relevant information openly and avoid withholding important details. This helps create a shared understanding of the context.

- Active Listening: Participants listen attentively to each other, seeking to understand the other person's perspective without judgment. This involves not only hearing the words spoken but also understanding the emotions and intentions behind them.

- Vulnerability: Participants are willing to be open about their own thoughts and feelings, even if they make themselves vulnerable. This authenticity encourages others to do the same.

- Respect: Open and honest dialogue requires a respectful attitude toward others' opinions and experiences, even when there are disagreements. Respectful communication helps maintain a positive and constructive atmosphere.

- Empathy: Participants strive to understand and acknowledge each other's feelings and experiences. This helps build connections and fosters a sense of shared humanity.

- Constructive Feedback: Participants provide feedback in a constructive manner, focusing on specific behaviors or issues rather than making personal attacks. This allows for improvement without creating defensiveness.

- Clarity: Communication is clear and straightforward, minimizing misunderstandings. This involves using language that is easily understood and avoiding ambiguity.

Open and honest dialogue is crucial in various settings, including personal relationships, workplaces, and communities. It can lead to better problem-solving, stronger relationships, and a more positive and inclusive environment. Embracing this approach often requires a commitment from all parties involved to prioritize sincerity and authenticity in their communication.

Creating a safe space for discussion

Creating a safe space for discussion is crucial for fostering open and respectful communication. Here are some guidelines and tips to help establish and maintain a safe environment:

Establish Ground Rules:

- Clearly outline the purpose and goals of the discussion.

- Set ground rules for respectful communication.

- Encourage participants to listen actively and avoid interrupting.

Encourage Open-mindedness:

- Emphasize the importance of being open to different perspectives.

- Encourage participants to question their assumptions and consider alternative viewpoints.

Respect and Empathy:

- Stress the importance of respecting others' opinions, even if they differ.

- Promote empathy by asking participants to consider how others might feel about a particular issue.

Moderation:

- Have a moderator to guide the discussion and enforce ground rules.

- Intervene if the conversation becomes disrespectful or off-topic.

Inclusive Language:

- Encourage the use of inclusive and non-discriminatory language.

- Remind participants to be mindful of their words and avoid offensive language.

Provide a Platform for All Voices:

- Ensure that everyone has an opportunity to speak.

- Avoid letting a few dominant voices dominate the conversation.

Feedback Mechanism:

- Establish a mechanism for participants to provide feedback on the discussion process.

- Use feedback to make improvements and adjustments for future discussions.

Educational Resources:

- Share relevant resources to help participants understand different perspectives.

- Provide information that supports informed and constructive discussions.

Confidentiality:

- Make it clear that personal information shared during the discussion should remain confidential.

- Foster an environment where participants feel safe to express themselves without fear of judgment.

Addressing Conflict:

- Have a process for addressing conflicts or disagreements.

- Encourage participants to address the issue, not attack the person.

Encourage Constructive Criticism:

- Foster an atmosphere where participants feel comfortable providing constructive criticism.

- Highlight the value of feedback for personal and collective growth.

Follow Up:

- After the discussion, provide a summary or follow-up to reinforce key points.

- Check in with participants to gather additional feedback and assess the overall experience.

By implementing these guidelines, you can create a safe space for discussion where individuals feel comfortable expressing their thoughts and engaging in meaningful conversations.

Active listening techniques

Active listening is a communication skill that involves fully focusing, understanding, and responding to a speaker. It goes beyond simply hearing words; it requires engagement and empathy. Here are some active listening techniques:

Give Your Full Attention:

- Eliminate distractions and focus solely on the speaker.

- Put away electronic devices and turn off notifications.

Show That You're Listening:

- Use nonverbal cues such as nodding, maintaining eye contact, and leaning slightly forward.

- Use facial expressions to convey interest and understanding.

Paraphrase:

- Repeat what the speaker has said in your own words to ensure understanding.

- This also helps to clarify any misunderstandings and lets the speaker know you are actively engaged.

Reflect Feelings:

- Acknowledge and validate the speaker's emotions by expressing understanding of their feelings.

- For example, you might say, "It sounds like you're really frustrated about..."

Ask Clarifying Questions:

- Seek additional information to ensure a clear understanding.

- Open-ended questions encourage the speaker to elaborate and share more details.

Summarize:

- Periodically summarize the key points to demonstrate your comprehension and to check if you're on the same page.

Empathize:

- Put yourself in the speaker's shoes and try to understand their perspective.

- Express empathy by acknowledging their feelings and experiences.

Avoid Interrupting:

- Let the speaker finish their thoughts before responding.

- Avoid interrupting or finishing their sentences.

Use Positive Body Language:

- Maintain an open and inviting posture.

- Avoid crossing your arms, as it may convey defensiveness.

Provide Feedback:

- Offer feedback on what you've heard to confirm your understanding.

- For example, say, "It sounds like what you're saying is..."

Resist the Urge to Judge:

- Suspend judgment and avoid forming opinions prematurely.

- Create a safe space for the speaker to express themselves without fear of criticism.

Be Patient:

- Allow the speaker to take their time and express themselves at their own pace.

- Rushing the conversation can hinder effective communication.

By incorporating these active listening techniques into your communication style, you can enhance your ability to understand others, build stronger relationships, and contribute to more effective and meaningful conversations.

Identifying underlying issues

Identifying underlying issues in any situation typically involves a systematic and thoughtful approach. Here are some general steps you can take to identify underlying issues:

Define the Problem:

- Clearly articulate the problem or issue you are trying to address. Make sure you understand the scope and boundaries of the problem.

Gather Information:

- Collect relevant data and information related to the issue. This might involve conducting research, gathering input from stakeholders, or reviewing relevant documents.

Ask Questions:

- Pose questions to yourself and others to uncover additional layers of the problem. Ask "why" multiple times to dig deeper into the root causes.

Explore Different Perspectives:

- Consider various viewpoints and perspectives on the issue. Different stakeholders may have different insights into the problem, so it's essential to understand multiple angles.

Identify Patterns and Trends:

- Look for patterns or recurring themes in the data and information you've gathered. Identifying trends can help you understand the dynamics of the problem.

Use Problem-Solving Tools:

- Employ problem-solving tools and techniques, such as the 5 Whys, SWOT analysis, or fishbone diagrams (Ishikawa diagrams), to systematically analyze the problem.

Consider Interconnected Factors:

- Understand how different factors might be interconnected and influence each other. Sometimes, issues have multiple causes that interact in complex ways.

Examine External Influences:

- Consider external factors that may be impacting the situation. This could include economic, political, social, or technological influences.

Check for Assumptions:

- Question any assumptions you or others may have about the problem. Assumptions can sometimes lead to overlooking critical factors.

Prioritize Issues:

- Once you've identified multiple factors contributing to the problem, prioritize them based on their impact and feasibility of addressing them.

Seek Feedback:

- Discuss your findings and analysis with others, especially those who have expertise in the relevant area. External perspectives can provide valuable insights.

Continuous Iteration:

- The process of identifying underlying issues is often iterative. As you gather more information and implement solutions, revisit your understanding of the problem and adjust your approach accordingly.

Remember that identifying underlying issues is not a one-time task; it's an ongoing process that may require continuous refinement as you gain more insights and data.

Past traumas

If you're dealing with past traumas, it's crucial to acknowledge that the effects of trauma can be complex and impact various aspects of your life. Seeking support is an important step towards healing. Here are some general suggestions:

- Professional Help: Consider reaching out to a mental health professional such as a therapist, counselor, or psychologist. They can provide you with the tools and support needed to navigate through your past traumas.

- Supportive Relationships: Share your experiences with trusted friends, family members, or support groups. Having a strong support system can make a significant difference in the healing process.

- Self-Care: Prioritize self-care activities that promote your well-being, both physically and mentally. This may include regular exercise, meditation, journaling, or engaging in hobbies that bring you joy.

- Educate Yourself: Learn more about the effects of trauma and how it can manifest. Understanding your own reactions and behaviors can be empowering.

- Set Boundaries: Recognize and establish healthy boundaries in your relationships. Communicate your needs and limits to others and give yourself the space to prioritize your own well-being.

- Mindfulness and Relaxation Techniques: Practices like mindfulness meditation, deep breathing exercises, or yoga can help you manage stress and anxiety.

- Take Small Steps: Healing from trauma is a gradual process. Allow yourself the time and space to progress at a pace that feels comfortable for you.

Remember that everyone's journey toward healing is unique. If you're in an immediate crisis, please reach out to a crisis hotline or seek emergency help. Professional support can be instrumental in guiding you through the healing process.

Unmet needs and desires

Unmet needs and desires refer to the aspects of an individual's life that are not currently fulfilled or satisfied. These can encompass a wide range of areas, including physical, emotional, social, and psychological needs. Identifying and understanding unmet needs and desires is crucial for personal growth, well-being, and overall satisfaction. Here are some examples across different domains:

Physical Needs:

- Adequate nutrition, shelter, and healthcare.

- Regular exercise and physical activity.

Emotional Needs:

- Love and companionship.

- Recognition and validation.

- Emotional support and understanding.

Social Needs:

- Friendships and social connections.

- Feeling a sense of belonging and community.

- Opportunities for social interaction.

Psychological Needs:

- Personal development and self-improvement.

- Autonomy and a sense of control over one's life.

- Intellectual stimulation and learning.

Career and Achievement Needs:

- Job satisfaction and meaningful work.

- Recognition and appreciation for accomplishments.

- Opportunities for career advancement.

Creative and Recreational Needs:

- Outlets for creativity and self-expression.

- Leisure and recreational activities.

- Hobbies and interests.

Spiritual Needs:

- A sense of purpose and meaning in life.

- Connection to something greater than oneself.

- Spiritual exploration and growth.

Financial Needs:

- Financial security and stability.

- The ability to meet basic financial obligations.

- Opportunities for financial growth and prosperity.

Understanding unmet needs and desires is a personal and introspective process. It involves self-reflection, honest assessment, and sometimes seeking feedback from others. Once identified, individuals can take steps to address these unmet needs, whether through personal development, seeking support from others, or making changes in various aspects of their lives.

It's important to note that addressing unmet needs is an ongoing process, as individuals grow, and their circumstances change. Regular self-reflection and adaptation are essential for maintaining a fulfilling and satisfying life.

Chapter 10
RECONNECTING EMOTIONALLY

Reconnecting emotionally with someone is a delicate process that requires patience, understanding, and effective communication. Here are some general tips that may help:

Reflect on the Past:

- Consider what led to the emotional disconnection. Understanding the root causes can guide your efforts to reconnect.

Open Communication:

- Initiate an open and honest conversation. Share your feelings and encourage the other person to do the same. Be attentive and actively listen without judgment.

Express Yourself:

- Clearly articulate your emotions, needs, and desires. Use "I" statements to avoid sounding accusatory and to take responsibility for your feelings.

Apologize and Forgive:

- If necessary, apologize for any actions or words that may have contributed to the emotional distance. Be willing to forgive and seek forgiveness if applicable.

Quality Time:

- Spend quality time together. Engage in activities you both enjoy creating positive experiences and memories.

Show Empathy:

- Understand the other person's perspective and validate their feelings. Empathy goes a long way in rebuilding emotional connections.

Be Patient:

- Reconnecting emotionally is a process that takes time. Be patient and allow the relationship to naturally evolve.

Seek Professional Help:

- If the emotional distance is significant or if communication breaks down, consider seeking the help of a therapist or counselor. Professional guidance can provide valuable insights and strategies.

Work on Yourself:

- Sometimes, personal growth is essential for emotional reconnection. Assess your own behaviors and attitudes and be willing to make positive changes.

Shared Goals:

- Identify common goals and aspirations. Working together towards shared objectives can strengthen your emotional bond.

Celebrate Achievements:

- Acknowledge and celebrate each other's accomplishments, no matter how small. Positive reinforcement can enhance emotional connections.

Maintain Respect:

- Treat each other with respect, even in times of disagreement. Respect is a foundation for a healthy emotional connection.

Remember that every relationship is unique, and the approach may vary based on the individuals involved. Open communication, empathy, and a commitment to understanding each other's needs are key components of emotional reconnection.

Rekindling intimacy

Rekindling intimacy in a relationship can be a rewarding and fulfilling process. Here are some suggestions to help you and your partner reconnect on a deeper level:

Communication:

- Open and honest communication is crucial. Share your feelings, desires, and concerns with each other.

- Actively listen to your partner without judgment and make an effort to understand their perspective.

Quality Time:

- Spend quality time together doing activities you both enjoy. This could be as simple as cooking together, going for a walk, or having a movie night.

- Be present in the moment and avoid distractions, such as phone calls or work-related matters.

Romantic Gestures:

- Surprise your partner with small, thoughtful gestures. It could be a love note, a special dinner, or a meaningful gift.

- Revisit the activities or places that hold sentimental value for both of you.

Physical Touch:

- Physical touch is a powerful way to rekindle intimacy. Hold hands, cuddle, or simply hug each other.

- Explore each other's needs and desires in terms of physical intimacy and be open to trying new things together.

Express Gratitude:

- Express appreciation for your partner regularly. Acknowledge their efforts and qualities that you admire.

- Cultivate a positive atmosphere by focusing on the positive aspects of your relationship.

Shared Goals:

- Discuss and set common goals for the future. This could be related to personal growth, career, or shared experiences.

- Working towards common objectives can strengthen your bond and rekindle the sense of partnership.

Rediscover Each Other:

- Take the time to learn about each other again. People change, and interests may evolve over time. Ask questions and be genuinely curious about your partner's thoughts and feelings.

Seek Professional Help:

- If communication and intimacy issues persist, consider seeking the help of a relationship counselor or therapist. They can provide guidance and facilitate productive conversations.

Build Trust:

- Trust is the foundation of a strong relationship. Work on rebuilding and strengthening trust through open communication and consistent actions.

Self-Care:

- Take care of yourself physically and emotionally. When you are in a good place individually, it can positively impact your relationship.

Remember that rekindling intimacy is a gradual process, and it requires effort and commitment from both partners. Be patient with each other and celebrate the progress you make together.

Emotional bonding exercises

Emotional bonding exercises can be valuable in strengthening connections between individuals, whether in romantic relationships, friendships, or family. Here are some exercises that can help foster emotional intimacy:

Share Appreciations:

- Take turns expressing specific things you appreciate about each other.

- Be genuine and specific in your compliments.

Deep Listening:

- Set aside dedicated time for one-on-one conversations.

- Practice active listening—give your full attention, make eye contact, and refrain from interrupting.

Life Timeline:

- Share significant events from your life with each other.

- Discuss how these experiences have shaped you and impacted your values.

Vulnerability Circle:

- Create a safe space to share your fears, insecurities, and vulnerabilities.

- Encourage openness and assure each other that judgments are not allowed.

Appreciation Letters:

- Write heartfelt letters expressing your appreciation for the other person.

- Exchange the letters and take time to read them aloud to each other.

Dream Building:

- Discuss your individual dreams and aspirations.

- Explore ways you can support each other in achieving those dreams.

Gratitude Journal:

- Keep a joint gratitude journal where you both write down things you are thankful for.

- Share your entries with each other regularly.

Memory Lane:

- Look through old photos or mementos together.

- Reminisce about shared experiences and the journey you've taken together.

Mindfulness Exercises:

- Practice mindfulness or meditation together to deepen your connection.

- This can include activities like deep breathing or guided meditation.

Role Reversal:

- Take turns expressing how you perceive the other person's emotions and thoughts.

- This exercise can enhance empathy and understanding.

Bucket List Creation:

- Create a bucket list of activities or experiences you both want to share.

- Make plans to fulfill these items over time.

Shared Goals:

- Identify common goals and aspirations.

- Work together to outline steps to achieve these goals.

Empathy Building:

- Share personal stories that evoke empathy.

- Discuss how you can support each other in challenging times.

Random Acts of Kindness:

- Perform unexpected acts of kindness for each other.

- This can be a great way to express love and care in simple, meaningful ways.

Remember, the key to these exercises is openness, honesty, and a willingness to be vulnerable. Building emotional bonds takes time and effort, so be patient and committed to the process.

Rediscovering shared interests

- Rediscovering shared interests can be a wonderful way to strengthen connections with others. Here are some suggestions on how to go about it:

Reflect on Past Interests:

- Think about activities or hobbies you both enjoyed in the past. What were some things you used to do together that brought joy or excitement?

Open Communication:

- Initiate a conversation about shared memories and past activities. Ask the other person about their favorite memories or experiences together.

Explore New Interpretations:

- Consider revisiting old interests with a fresh perspective. For example, if you both used to enjoy hiking, try exploring new trails or hiking in a different season.

Try Something New Together:

- Discover new activities that align with both of your interests. This could be something neither of you has tried before, providing a novel and shared experience.

Attend Events:

- Look for events or gatherings related to your shared interests. Whether it's a concert, art exhibition, or sports game, attending such events can reignite the passion for shared activities.

Join a Club or Group:

- Find local clubs or groups centered around your shared interests. This can introduce you to new people who share the same passions and create a sense of community.

Take Classes or Workshops:

- Enroll in a class or workshop related to your shared interests. Learning something new together can be both enjoyable and educational.

Incorporate into Routine:

- Integrate your shared interests into your regular routine. This could be as simple as dedicating time each week to engage in the activities you both enjoy.

Be Open-Minded:

- Stay open-minded and be willing to compromise. It's possible that your interests may have evolved over time, so be receptive to trying new variations or combinations.

Celebrate Achievements:

- Acknowledge and celebrate each other's achievements related to your shared interests. This could be as small as completing a project or reaching a milestone.

Document and Share:

- Create a shared journal or blog where you document your experiences, thoughts, and memories related to your shared interests. This can serve as a keepsake and a way to stay connected.

Remember, the key is to approach the process with an open heart and a willingness to explore new possibilities together. Communication and a shared sense of enthusiasm can help reignite the joy of shared interests.

Couples therapy

Couples therapy, also known as marriage or relationship counseling, is a form of psychotherapy that aims to help couples resolve conflicts and improve their relationship. It involves working with a trained therapist to explore and understand the dynamics within the relationship, identify areas of concern, and develop strategies to enhance communication and intimacy.

Here are some key aspects of couple's therapy:

- Communication Skills: A significant focus of couples therapy is often on improving communication. Therapists help couples learn effective communication skills, including active listening, expressing emotions, and resolving conflicts constructively.

- Conflict Resolution: Couples therapy addresses specific issues and conflicts that may be causing distress within the relationship. The therapist helps the couple understand the root causes of their conflicts and guides them in finding mutually satisfactory solutions.

- Understanding Patterns: Therapists often help couples identify and understand recurring patterns of behavior or communication that contribute to relationship difficulties. This can involve exploring family-of-origin issues, cultural influences, and individual personality traits.

- Building Intimacy: Couples therapy aims to strengthen emotional and physical intimacy. Therapists may suggest exercises or activities that promote connection and closeness between partners.

- Setting Goals: Couples often work with therapists to establish realistic and achievable goals for their relationship. These goals may include improved communication, rebuilding trust, or addressing specific issues like parenting or financial management.

- Preventing Future Issues: In addition to addressing current concerns, couples therapy may also focus on providing tools and strategies for preventing future conflicts. This proactive approach can help couples develop skills to navigate challenges as they arise.

- Individual Issues: Sometimes, individual issues contribute to relationship problems. Couples therapy can address how each person's individual experiences, beliefs, or traumas impact the relationship.

- Assessment and Diagnosis: In some cases, therapists may use assessment tools to gather information about the couple's relationship and individual factors. This information can help guide the therapeutic process.

It's important to note that the success of couples therapy often depends on the willingness of both partners to actively participate and commit to the process. Additionally, finding a skilled and experienced therapist is crucial. Couples therapy can be beneficial for a variety of issues, including communication problems, infidelity, trust issues, and major life transitions. If you and your partner are considering couples therapy, it may be helpful to research and choose a qualified therapist who fits your needs.

Sex therapy

Sex therapy is a form of psychotherapy that focuses on addressing issues related to sexuality and sexual function. It is provided by licensed mental health professionals who have specialized training in the field of sex therapy. Sex therapists work with individuals or couples to help them explore and understand their sexual concerns, improve communication, and enhance their overall sexual satisfaction.

Here are some common reasons why individuals or couples seek sex therapy:

- Communication Issues: Difficulty discussing sexual needs and desires with a partner.

- Intimacy Concerns: Challenges in establishing or maintaining emotional and physical intimacy.

- Performance Anxiety: Anxiety or concerns related to sexual performance.

- Desire Discrepancy: Differences in sexual desire between partners.

- Erectile Dysfunction or Premature Ejaculation: Sexual dysfunctions that can impact a person's or a couple's sexual satisfaction.

- Pain During Sex: Physical discomfort or pain during sexual activities.

- Past Trauma: Previous sexual trauma or abuse that affects current sexual functioning.

- Sexual Orientation or Identity Concerns: Exploration of one's sexual orientation or gender identity.

- During sex therapy sessions, therapists use various therapeutic techniques to address the specific concerns of the individual or couple. These may include:

- Education: Providing information about sexual anatomy, response, and functioning.

- Communication Skills: Teaching effective communication strategies to discuss sexual issues openly and honestly.

- Behavioral Interventions: Implementing exercises or homework assignments to address specific sexual concerns.

- Cognitive Restructuring: Identifying and challenging negative thoughts or beliefs related to sex.

- Sensate Focus: Gradual, structured touching exercises to enhance physical and emotional intimacy.

- It's important to note that sex therapy is a confidential and non-judgmental space where individuals or couples can explore their concerns without fear of stigma. If you are considering sex therapy, it's recommended to seek out a licensed and certified sex therapist who has received specialized training in the field.

If you are looking for a sex therapist, you can contact professional organizations like the American Association of Sexuality Educators, Counselors, and Therapists (AASECT) or other relevant national or regional associations to find qualified professionals.

Chapter 11

OVERCOMING PHYSICAL CHALLENGES

Overcoming physical challenges can be a significant and empowering journey that requires resilience, adaptability, and a positive mindset. Whether facing a disability, injury, or chronic condition, individuals can take steps to enhance their quality of life and achieve their goals. Here are some general strategies for overcoming physical challenges:

Acceptance and Positive Mindset:

- Acceptance of the situation is the first step. Embrace your current reality and focus on what you can control.

- Cultivate a positive mindset to help you approach challenges with optimism and resilience.

Seek Support:

- Build a strong support system with friends, family, and professionals who can provide emotional support, encouragement, and practical assistance.

- Consider joining support groups or communities where you can connect with others facing similar challenges.

Professional Guidance:

- Consult with healthcare professionals, rehabilitation specialists, physical therapists, and occupational therapists to develop personalized plans for recovery or adaptation.

- Explore assistive devices or technologies that can enhance your independence and functionality.

Adaptation and Innovation:

- Embrace adaptive strategies and tools that can help you perform daily tasks or engage in activities you enjoy.

- Stay informed about new technologies and innovations that may improve your quality of life.

Set Realistic Goals:

- Establish short-term and long-term goals that are realistic and achievable. Celebrate small victories along the way to maintain motivation.

- Break down larger goals into smaller, manageable tasks to make progress more achievable.

Physical Activity:

- Engage in physical activities that are suitable for your abilities. Regular exercise can improve physical and mental well-being.

- Consult with healthcare professionals to develop a safe and effective exercise routine.

Mind-Body Connection:

- Explore practices that enhance the mind-body connection, such as meditation, yoga, or tai chi, to promote overall well-being.

- Focus on activities that bring joy and relaxation, helping to alleviate stress and improve mental health.

Education and Advocacy:

- Educate yourself about your condition and available resources. Knowledge empowers you to make informed decisions.

- Advocate for yourself and others facing similar challenges to promote awareness and accessibility.

Build Resilience:

- Develop coping strategies to manage stress and adversity. Resilience is crucial for navigating the ups and downs of life.

- Consider seeking counseling or therapy to address emotional aspects of overcoming physical challenges.

Celebrate Achievements:

- Acknowledge and celebrate your achievements, no matter how small. Recognizing progress can boost confidence and motivation.

Remember that everyone's journey is unique, and the strategies employed will vary based on individual circumstances. Adaptability and a proactive approach can go a long way in overcoming physical challenges and leading a fulfilling life.

Physical examinations

Physical examinations are a crucial aspect of healthcare that involve a thorough assessment of an individual's overall health and well-being. These examinations are typically conducted by healthcare professionals, such as physicians, nurses, or other qualified healthcare providers. The primary goals of a physical examination are to:

- Assess General Health: The examiner will evaluate various aspects of the individual's health, including vital signs such as blood pressure, heart rate, respiratory rate, and temperature.

- Screen for Diseases: Physical examinations often involve screenings to detect potential health problems early on. This may include checking for signs of diseases such as hypertension, diabetes, or cancer.

- Review Medical History: Healthcare providers will inquire about the individual's medical history, including any current or past illnesses, surgeries, medications, and family medical history.

- Examine Organ Systems: A comprehensive physical examination involves the assessment of different organ systems, including the cardiovascular, respiratory, gastrointestinal, musculoskeletal, and neurological systems.

- Check Body Mass Index (BMI): BMI is often calculated to assess whether an individual is underweight, normal weight, overweight, or obese. This can be an indicator of potential health risks.

- Evaluate Mental Health: In addition to physical health, some physical examinations include assessments of mental health, such as screening for depression, anxiety, or cognitive function.

- Perform Specialized Examinations: Depending on the individual's age, gender, and specific health concerns, additional examinations may be conducted. For example, a pelvic exam and breast exam for women, or a prostate exam for men.

- Immunization Review: The healthcare provider may review the individual's immunization status and recommend vaccinations if needed.

- Provide Counseling: During the examination, healthcare providers may offer advice on lifestyle factors such as diet, exercise, and stress management. They may also discuss preventive measures and screen for risky behaviors like smoking or excessive alcohol consumption.

- Patient Education: Physical examinations are also opportunities for patient education. Healthcare providers may explain test results, discuss preventive measures, and address any questions or concerns the individual may have.

It's important to note that the specific components of a physical examination can vary based on factors such as age, gender, medical history, and the reason for the visit. Additionally, advancements in technology and telemedicine have led to the development of virtual physical examinations, where certain aspects of the assessment may be conducted remotely.

Regular physical examinations are essential for maintaining good health, preventing diseases, and addressing health issues in their early stages when they are often more treatable. Individuals should schedule routine check-ups with their healthcare providers and communicate openly about their health concerns.

Lifestyle changes

Lifestyle changes can have a profound impact on your overall well-being. Whether you're looking to improve your physical health, mental well-being, or overall quality of life, making positive lifestyle changes can make a significant difference. Here are some common areas where people often consider making lifestyle changes:

Physical Activity:

- Incorporate regular exercise into your routine, aiming for at least 150 minutes of moderate-intensity aerobic activity per week.

- Find activities you enjoy, whether it's walking, running, cycling, swimming, or dancing.

Healthy Eating:

- Focus on a balanced diet with a variety of fruits, vegetables, whole grains, lean proteins, and healthy fats.

- Pay attention to portion sizes and try to minimize processed and sugary foods.

Sleep:

- Aim for 7-9 hours of quality sleep each night.

- Establish a consistent sleep schedule and create a relaxing bedtime routine.

- Stress Management:

- Practice stress-reducing techniques such as meditation, deep breathing, yoga, or mindfulness.

- Identify sources of stress and find healthy ways to cope with it.

Hydration:

- Drink an adequate amount of water throughout the day to stay hydrated.

- Limit the intake of sugary drinks and excessive caffeine.

Social Connections:

- Cultivate and maintain positive relationships with friends and family.

- Spend time with loved ones and engage in social activities.

Mental Health:

- Prioritize mental health by seeking professional help if needed.

- Practice self-care and take breaks when necessary.

Hobbies and Recreation:

- Engage in activities you enjoy promoting relaxation and creativity.

- Take time for hobbies and leisure activities to balance work and personal life.

Limiting Unhealthy Habits:

- Reduce or quit smoking and limit alcohol consumption.

- Be mindful of excessive screen time and sedentary behavior.

Financial Health:

- Develop and stick to a budget to reduce financial stress.

- Save for the future and set financial goals.

Continuous Learning:

- Embrace a mindset of lifelong learning to stimulate intellectual well-being.

- Explore new interests and challenges.

Environmental Awareness:

- Consider eco-friendly practices to contribute to a healthier planet.

- Connect with nature and spend time outdoors.

Remember, lifestyle changes are most effective when they are gradual and sustainable. It's important to set realistic goals and celebrate small victories along the way. Additionally, consulting with healthcare professionals or specialists in relevant areas can provide personalized guidance based on your individual needs and health status.

Experimenting with intimacy

It's important to approach any experimentation with intimacy with respect, communication, and consent. Intimacy can mean different things to different people, so it's crucial to understand your own boundaries and the boundaries of your partner(s). Here are some general tips for experimenting with intimacy:

- Communication: Open and honest communication is key. Discuss your desires, boundaries, and expectations with your partner(s) before experimenting. Make sure everyone is on the same page and comfortable with the proposed activities.

- Consent: Always prioritize consent. Consent should be enthusiastic, ongoing, and informed. It's crucial that everyone involved feels comfortable and willingly participates. If anyone expresses discomfort or withdraws consent at any point, stop the activity immediately.

- Start Slow: Begin with activities that are less intense and gradually work your way up. This allows everyone to gauge their comfort levels and ensures a positive experience.

- Educate Yourself: If you're exploring new aspects of intimacy, take the time to educate yourself about the activities you're interested in. This can help you understand potential risks, safety measures, and proper techniques.

- Respect Boundaries: Everyone has different comfort levels and boundaries. Be attentive to your partner's cues and communicate openly about what feels good and what doesn't. Always respect each other's limits.

- Create a Safe Space: Ensure that the physical and emotional environment is safe and comfortable. This includes using protection if necessary and being aware of the emotional well-being of everyone involved.

- Check-In: During and after the experience, check in with your partner(s) about their feelings. Open communication allows everyone to process the experience and address any concerns or feelings that may arise.

- Self-Care: Take care of your own well-being and be mindful of your emotional and physical state. If something doesn't feel right, it's okay to express your feelings and take a step back.

- Variety of Intimacy: Intimacy doesn't just refer to physical activities. Emotional intimacy, communication, and shared experiences are equally important. Explore different facets of intimacy to strengthen your connection with your partner(s).

- Professional Guidance: If you're exploring more complex or potentially risky activities, consider seeking advice from a professional, such as a sex educator or therapist. They can provide guidance on safety, communication, and consent.

The key is to prioritize the well-being and comfort of everyone involved. Consent and communication are crucial in creating a positive and respectful intimate experience.

Trying new activities together

Trying new activities together can be a great way to bond, create shared memories, and discover common interests. Whether you're in a new relationship or looking to spice things up in a long-term one, here are some ideas for trying new activities together:

- Cooking Class: Take a cooking class together to learn new recipes and cooking techniques. It's a fun and interactive way to bond while enjoying delicious food.

- Outdoor Adventures: Go on a hike, bike ride, or try a new outdoor activity like kayaking, rock climbing, or zip-lining. Nature provides a beautiful backdrop for shared experiences.

- Art or Craft Workshop: Explore your creative side by taking an art or craft workshop. This could include painting, pottery, or even a DIY home decor class.

- Dance Lessons: Sign up for a dance class, whether it's ballroom, salsa, or swing. Learning to dance together can be a playful and intimate experience.

- Escape Room: Challenge yourselves with an escape room adventure. This activity promotes teamwork and problem-solving skills while providing a thrilling experience.

- Cultural Events: Attend a live performance, such as a play, concert, or ballet. Experiencing the arts together can be both entertaining and thought-provoking.

- Volunteer Together: Find a cause you both care about and volunteer together. This not only helps others but also strengthens your connection as a couple.

- Fitness Class: Try a new fitness class together, whether it's yoga, spin, or a high-intensity workout. It's a healthy and energizing way to spend time together.

- Travel to a New Place: Explore a new city or country together. Traveling allows you to experience different cultures, cuisines, and landscapes.

- Board Game Night: Have a board game or puzzle night at home. It's a low-key way to enjoy each other's company and engage in friendly competition.

- Wine or Beer Tasting: Visit a local winery or brewery and sample different varieties together. It can be a fun and educational experience, and you might discover new favorites.

- Photography Excursion: Take a photography class or simply explore a new area with cameras in hand. Capture moments and create a shared photo album.

The key is to choose activities that align with both of your interests and comfort levels. The goal is to have fun, deepen your connection, and create lasting memories together.

Exploring each other's fantasies

Exploring each other's fantasies can be a healthy and exciting way to enhance intimacy and connection in a relationship. Here are some tips on how to approach this:

Establish Trust and Communication:

- Ensure that you and your partner feel safe and secure discussing fantasies without judgment.

- Open and honest communication is crucial. Create a space where both of you can express desires without fear of criticism.

Start Slow:

- Begin with smaller, less intense fantasies to ease into the conversation. This helps build comfort and understanding between partners.

- Share fantasies that you are comfortable discussing and encourage your partner to do the same.

Respect Boundaries:

- Establish clear boundaries and respect each other's limits. Not every fantasy needs to be acted upon, and it's important to prioritize mutual comfort.

Fantasy Exploration Together:

- Identify fantasies that you both find intriguing and explore them together. This shared experience can deepen your connection and create lasting memories.

Use Imaginative Language:

- Describe fantasies using sensual and creative language. This can help create a vivid mental image for your partner and enhance the experience of discussing fantasies.

Be Open-Minded:

- Approach your partner's fantasies with an open mind. Even if a fantasy is not something you would have considered, be willing to understand and discuss it without judgment.

Consider Role-Playing:

- If both partners are comfortable, consider incorporating role-playing into your exploration. This can add an element of playfulness and excitement.

Regularly Check-In:

- As with any aspect of a relationship, it's important to regularly check in with each other about your comfort levels and feelings. Feelings and boundaries can change over time.

Educate Yourself:

- Take the time to learn about your partner's fantasies and desires. Understanding the context and emotions behind a fantasy can foster a deeper connection.

Professional Guidance:

- If you encounter challenges or if a fantasy involves elements that might be difficult to navigate, consider seeking professional guidance, such as couples counseling or sex therapy.

Remember that everyone is unique, and what works for one couple may not work for another. The key is to prioritize open communication, mutual respect, and a shared commitment to maintaining a healthy and fulfilling relationship.

Chapter 12

REDISCOVERING PASSION

Rediscovering passion can be a fulfilling and transformative journey. Here are some steps you can consider reigniting your passion:

Reflect on Your Interests:

- Take some time to reflect on your interests and hobbies. What activities used to bring you joy and excitement? Make a list of things that you used to be passionate about.

Explore New Activities:

- Trying out new activities can help you discover new passions. Attend workshops, classes, or events related to your interests. Stepping out of your comfort zone can open up new possibilities.

Reconnect with Old Hobbies:

- Revisit activities you used to love but may have neglected over time. Whether it's playing a musical instrument, painting, or a sport, rekindling old hobbies can revive your passion.

Set Goals:

- Define clear and achievable goals related to your passions. Having specific objectives can provide direction and motivation. Break down larger goals into smaller, manageable tasks to make progress more attainable.

Surround Yourself with Inspiration:

- Immerse yourself in environments that inspire you. Attend events, read books, or follow individuals who share similar passions. Exposure to passion-driven content can reignite your own enthusiasm.

Challenge Yourself:

- Push your boundaries and take on challenges. Overcoming obstacles and achieving goals can boost your confidence and reignite your passion. Embrace a growth mindset and view challenges as opportunities for learning and growth.

Create a Routine:

- Establish a routine that incorporates your passions. Dedicate specific times in your schedule for activities you love. Consistency can help cultivate and sustain your enthusiasm over time.

Collaborate with Others:

- Join communities or groups that share your interests. Collaborating with like-minded individuals can provide support, motivation, and fresh perspectives. It can also be an avenue for learning new things.

Practice Mindfulness:

- Be present in the moment and savor the experience of engaging in your passions. Mindfulness can deepen your connection to the activity and enhance the pleasure you derive from it.

Embrace Change:

- Be open to evolving interests and passions. As you grow and change, your passions may also shift. Embrace new possibilities and be willing to explore different avenues.

Seek Professional Guidance:

- If you're struggling to rediscover your passion or facing obstacles, consider seeking the guidance of a coach or therapist. They can provide insights, support, and strategies to help you navigate this journey.

Remember, rediscovering passion is a personal and ongoing process. It's about connecting with what truly excites and fulfills you. Be patient with yourself and enjoy the exploration of rediscovering your passions.

Spicing up the relationship

Spicing up a relationship is a great way to keep things exciting and maintain a strong connection with your partner. Here are some ideas to add a spark to your relationship:

Surprise Dates:

- Plan surprise dates or activities that your partner enjoys. It could be a spontaneous weekend getaway, a picnic in the park, or a themed date night at home.

Try New Hobbies Together:

- Explore new activities or hobbies together. This could be anything from cooking classes and dance lessons to hiking or painting.

Express Appreciation:

- Regularly express gratitude and appreciation for your partner. Small gestures, like leaving love notes or sending thoughtful texts, can go a long way in making your partner feel valued.

Spontaneity:

- Embrace spontaneity in your relationship. Sometimes, the most memorable moments happen when you least expect them.

Communication:

- Open and honest communication is crucial. Discuss your desires, dreams, and even fantasies with your partner. This helps build trust and intimacy.

Intimacy:

- Keep the physical intimacy alive. Try new things in the bedroom, explore each other's desires, and communicate openly about your needs.

Shared Goals:

- Set goals together, whether they are personal, professional, or relationship oriented. Working towards common objectives can strengthen your bond.

Travel Together:

- If possible, plan trips together. Exploring new places and experiencing different cultures can create lasting memories and deepen your connection.

Quality Time:

- Make sure to spend quality time together without distractions. Put away your phones and be fully present with each other.

Surprise Gifts:

- Give surprise gifts to show your love and appreciation. It doesn't have to be extravagant; even small, thoughtful gifts can make a big impact.

Laugh Together:

- Laughter is a great way to connect. Watch a funny movie, attend a comedy show, or reminisce about amusing moments from your past.

Role Play:

- Add a bit of excitement by engaging in role play. This can be a fun way to explore new aspects of your relationship and fantasies.

Shared Adventures:

- Take on new challenges or adventures together, whether it's trying a new sport, taking a class, or volunteering for a cause you both care about.

Create Traditions:

- Establishing traditions, whether it's a weekly movie night or an annual getaway, can create a sense of continuity and stability in your relationship.

Remember that every relationship is unique, so it's essential to tailor these suggestions to fit you and your partner's preferences. Communication is key, so make sure to discuss your ideas and desires openly with each other.

Introducing variety in the bedroom

Introducing variety in the bedroom can help keep things exciting and enhance your intimate relationship. Here are some ideas to add spice and variety to your bedroom activities:

Communication is Key:

- Talk openly with your partner about your desires, fantasies, and boundaries. Establishing clear communication is crucial for a healthy and satisfying intimate life.

Try New Positions:

- Experiment with different sexual positions to keep things interesting. There are countless positions that can add novelty and excitement to your intimate moments.

Explore Fantasies:

- Share your sexual fantasies with your partner and be open to exploring them together. Make sure both partners are comfortable and consensual in trying new things.

Role-Playing:

Engage in role-playing scenarios to add a sense of fantasy and excitement. Dressing up in costumes or assuming different personas can be a fun way to explore new dynamics.

Introduce Sensory Play:

- Experiment with sensory experiences, such as using blindfolds, feathers, or ice cubes. Heightening the senses can intensify pleasure and create a more immersive experience.

Incorporate Toys:

- Introduce adult toys or accessories into your intimate activities. This can include vibrators, handcuffs, or other items that can enhance pleasure for both partners.

Take Turns Initiating:

- Share the responsibility of initiating intimacy. This can help balance the power dynamics and ensure that both partners feel desired.

Surprise Your Partner:

- Plan surprises for your partner, whether it's a romantic evening, a weekend getaway, or a special date. The element of surprise can add excitement to your relationship.

Set the Mood:

- Create a sensual atmosphere with candles, soft lighting, and music. Setting the mood can enhance the overall experience and make it more memorable.

Schedule Intimate Time:

- Sometimes, life gets busy, and intimate moments may take a back seat. Schedule time for intimacy to ensure that it remains a priority in your relationship.

Take a Class Together:

- Consider attending a workshop or class on intimacy together. This can be a fun and educational way to explore new techniques and ideas.

Be Open to Experimentation:

- Be open-minded and willing to try new things. It's essential to create a safe and non-judgmental space where both partners feel comfortable expressing their desires.

The key is to maintain open communication, mutual consent, and a genuine desire to explore and connect with your partner. Every couple is unique, so find what works best for you both and enjoy the journey of discovering new aspects of your intimacy.

Romantic gestures and surprises

Romantic gestures and surprises can add excitement and depth to a relationship, showing your partner that you care and appreciate them. Here are some ideas:

Love Notes or Letters:

- Leave sweet notes in unexpected places, such as in their wallet, on the bathroom mirror, or in their lunch bag.

- Write a heartfelt letter expressing your feelings and leave it somewhere for them to find.

Surprise Dates:

- Plan a surprise date or weekend getaway. Choose activities or places that have sentimental value or are meaningful to your relationship.

- Create a scavenger hunt that leads to a special place or a gift.

Cook a Special Meal:

- Prepare their favorite meal or try cooking something new together.

- Create a romantic atmosphere with candles, soft music, and a beautifully set table.

Memory Lane:

- Create a scrapbook or photo album highlighting your favorite memories together.

- Reminisce about the early days of your relationship and recreate your first date.

Unexpected Gifts:

- Surprise them with a thoughtful and meaningful gift, even if it's small.

- Consider personalized items, such as custom jewelry or a monogrammed item.

Acts of Service:

- Take care of a task or responsibility that your partner finds burdensome.

- Offer to do something they enjoy but might not have the time for, like a hobby or a favorite activity.

Spontaneous Affection:

- Show physical affection unexpectedly, such as a hug, kiss, or holding hands.

- Surprise them with a gentle massage or a warm bath after a long day.

Create a Playlist:

- Make a playlist of songs that are meaningful to your relationship or that your partner enjoys.

- Play the playlist during a quiet evening together or on a road trip.

Thoughtful Surprises:

- Send flowers or a thoughtful gift to their workplace.

- Organize a surprise party with close friends and family to celebrate a special occasion.

Star Gazing:

- Plan a night of star gazing. Find a quiet spot away from city lights, bring a blanket, and enjoy the beauty of the night sky together.

Remember, the most meaningful gestures often come from knowing your partner well and tailoring surprises to their preferences and personality. Communication is key, so pay attention to what makes your partner happy and feel loved.

Cultivating ongoing connection

Cultivating ongoing connections, whether in personal relationships, professional networks, or communities, is crucial for building meaningful and sustainable interactions. Here are some general principles that can help foster ongoing connections:

Communication:

- Active Listening: Pay attention and show genuine interest in what others are saying. This helps build understanding and empathy.

- Clear Expression: Communicate your thoughts and feelings openly and honestly. Clarity promotes understanding.

Consistency:

- Regular Check-Ins: Stay in touch regularly, even if it's a simple message or a brief catch-up. Consistent communication reinforces the connection.

- Follow-Up: If you've discussed something, follow up on it. This shows commitment and reliability.

Reciprocity:

- Give and Take: Healthy relationships involve a balance of giving and receiving. Contribute to the relationship in ways that are meaningful to both parties.

- Support: Offer support when needed and be open to receiving support when you require it.

Shared Experiences:

- Create Memories: Participate in activities or share experiences together. This creates a shared history, strengthening the bond.

- Celebrate Successes: Acknowledge and celebrate achievements, both big and small.

Empathy:

- Understanding Perspectives: Put yourself in the other person's shoes. Understand their feelings, thoughts, and perspectives.

- Validation: Validate the other person's experiences and emotions. It fosters a sense of understanding and connection.

Adaptability:

- Flexibility: Be open to change and adapt to evolving circumstances. Life is dynamic, and flexibility is key to navigating challenges together.

- Learning and Growth: Encourage personal and mutual growth. Support each other's aspirations and provide constructive feedback.

Respect:

- Boundaries: Respect personal boundaries and be mindful of individual preferences.

- Appreciation: Express gratitude and appreciation for the qualities and contributions of others.

Shared Values:

- Identify Common Ground: Shared values create a foundation for a strong connection. Identify and nurture common interests and beliefs.

Conflict Resolution:

- Open Dialogue: Address conflicts through open and respectful communication. Avoiding conflicts can lead to resentment.

- Resolution: Work together to find solutions and compromises. Learn from conflicts to strengthen relationships.

Patience:

- Understanding Growth: Recognize that relationships evolve over time. Be patient during challenging phases, allowing for growth and development.

Remember that each relationship is unique, and these principles may need to be adjusted based on the context and individuals involved. Regular reflection and feedback can also contribute to the ongoing health of connections.

Regular date nights

Regular date nights can be a wonderful way to strengthen and maintain a romantic relationship. Here are some benefits and tips for incorporating regular date nights into your routine:

Benefits of Regular Date Nights:

- Connection: Date nights provide an opportunity for couples to connect on a deeper level, fostering emotional intimacy.

- Communication: Spending quality time together allows for open communication and the chance to discuss important topics outside the daily routine.

- Stress Relief: Date nights can be a break from the stresses of everyday life, providing a chance to relax and enjoy each other's company.

- Romance: A well-planned date night can bring back the romance and excitement that may fade over time in a relationship.

- Fun and Laughter: Engaging in enjoyable activities together promotes laughter and fun, creating positive memories.

Tips for Successful Date Nights:

- Schedule Regularly: Set a consistent schedule for date nights, whether it's once a week or once a month. Consistency is key.

- Quality Over Quantity: It's not just about the frequency but the quality of the time spent together. Focus on meaningful activities that you both enjoy.

- Switch It Up: Don't be afraid to try new things. Explore different restaurants, activities, or even take turns planning the date to keep things fresh.

- Put Away Devices: Make a conscious effort to disconnect from phones and other devices during your date. This allows you to be present and engaged with each other.

- Be Spontaneous: While having a planned date night is great, being spontaneous from time to time can add an element of surprise and excitement.

- Share Responsibilities: If possible, share responsibilities for planning and organizing date nights. This can help prevent one person from feeling overwhelmed or burdened.

- Create a Romantic Atmosphere: Whether you're staying in or going out, add some romantic touches to create a special atmosphere. This could include candles, music, or other elements that enhance the mood.

- Reflect and Connect: Take some time during the date to reflect on your relationship, express appreciation for each other, and discuss your dreams and goals.

Remember that the key is to prioritize and invest time in your relationship. Regular date nights can contribute to a healthy, happy, and lasting connection between partners.

Continual communication and check-ins

Continual communication and check-ins are essential elements in various contexts, including relationships, work environments, and project management. Here are some insights on how continual communication and check-ins can be valuable:

Workplace Environment:

Team Collaboration:

- Regular check-ins foster a sense of teamwork and collaboration.

- Team members can update each other on progress, share ideas, and address any challenges.

Feedback Loop:

- Continual communication provides a consistent feedback loop for employees.

- It allows for the timely identification and resolution of issues or concerns.

Alignment with Goals:

- Regular check-ins help ensure that individual and team efforts align with organizational goals.

- Any deviations can be addressed promptly to keep the team on track.

Motivation and Engagement:

- Frequent communication helps maintain high levels of motivation and engagement.

- Recognition and encouragement can be provided more regularly.

Project Management:

Progress Tracking:

- Regular check-ins facilitate tracking project progress.

- Milestones and deliverables can be reviewed to ensure they align with project timelines.

Risk Mitigation:

- Constant communication helps identify and address potential risks early on.

- This proactive approach can prevent minor issues from turning into major problems.

Resource Allocation:

- Check-ins allow for discussions on resource allocation and redistribution as needed.

- Teams can adjust priorities based on changing project requirements.

Adaptability:

- In dynamic environments, continual communication allows teams to adapt quickly to changes.

- Agile methodologies often incorporate frequent check-ins for this purpose.

Relationships:

Understanding and Empathy:

- Regular communication in relationships promotes understanding and empathy.

- Partners can address concerns and celebrate achievements together.

Conflict Resolution:

- Frequent check-ins help identify and resolve conflicts before they escalate.

- Open communication fosters a healthier and more resilient relationship.

Shared Growth:

- Couples, friends, or family members can support each other's personal and collective growth through ongoing communication.

- Sharing goals and aspirations helps in aligning individual paths.

Continual communication and check-ins are vital for staying connected, ensuring alignment, addressing challenges promptly, and fostering a positive and collaborative environment, whether in the workplace or personal relationships. Regular communication helps build trust and creates a foundation for success.

Chapter 13
SPICE UP THE ROMANCE

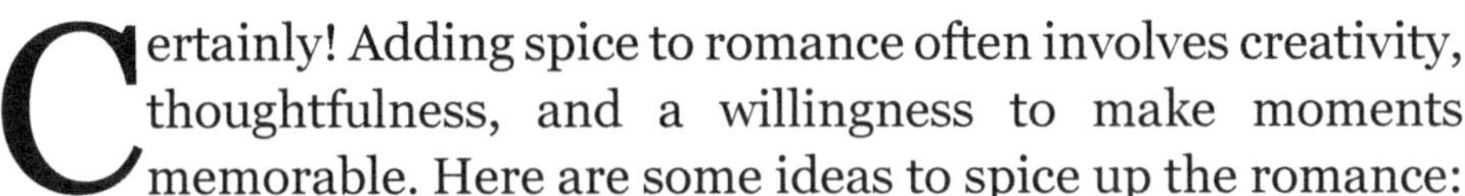

Certainly! Adding spice to romance often involves creativity, thoughtfulness, and a willingness to make moments memorable. Here are some ideas to spice up the romance:

- Surprise Dates: Plan unexpected dates to keep the excitement alive. It could be a picnic in the park, a rooftop dinner, or a spontaneous weekend getaway.

- Love Notes: Leave sweet notes in unexpected places — a heartfelt message in the bathroom mirror, a love letter in the car, or a post-it notes on the fridge.

- Cook Together: Prepare a romantic dinner together. Choose a recipe neither of you has tried before and enjoy the process of cooking together.

- Themed Evenings: Pick a theme for an evening — it could be a 'Movie Night,' 'Italian Night,' or 'Dancing Under the Stars.' Tailor your activities, food, and music to the chosen theme.

- Create a Memory Book: Compile photos, mementos, and notes that represent your journey together. This is a wonderful way to reminisce about your shared experiences.

- Adventure Together: Try something new together, whether it's a dance class, hiking, or a water sport. Sharing new experiences strengthens your bond.

- Spa Night: Create a spa-like atmosphere at home with scented candles, soothing music, and massage oils. Take turns pampering each other with massages.

- Random Acts of Kindness: Surprise your partner with small gestures of kindness, like bringing their favorite coffee, leaving a love note in their bag, or planning a surprise date.

- Dance Together: Clear a space in your living room, put on your favorite music, and dance together. It's a fun and intimate way to connect.

- Outdoor Adventure: If you both enjoy the outdoors, plan a camping trip, a hike to a scenic spot, or a beach day. Nature can be a beautiful backdrop for romance.

- Memory Lane: Visit places that hold sentimental value for both of you, such as where you first met or had your first date.

- Learn Something New Together: Take a class together, whether it's a cooking class, painting workshop, or dance lessons. Learning something new as a couple can be exciting and bonding.

The key to spicing up romance is to show thoughtfulness, attention, and a willingness to make the relationship a priority.

Tailor these ideas to your partner's preferences and interests for a personalized touch.

Surprise gestures

Surprise gestures can be a delightful way to express your feelings and make someone's day. Here are some ideas for surprise gestures:

Unexpected Gift:

Give a thoughtful gift for no particular reason. It could be something small that you know the person will appreciate.

Handwritten Note:

- Leave a heartfelt, handwritten note in a place where the person will find it. Express your feelings and appreciation.

Random Act of Kindness:

- Perform a random act of kindness, such as paying for someone's coffee or helping with a task without being asked.

Spontaneous Outing:

- Plan a surprise outing or activity that the person enjoys. It could be a picnic, a movie night, or a visit to a special place.

Personalized Playlist:

- Create a playlist of songs that hold significance for the person or that you think they'll enjoy. Share it with them unexpectedly.

Decorate Their Space:

- Decorate their workspace or living area with balloons, flowers, or other decorations to brighten their day.

Cook a Surprise Meal:

- Prepare a special meal or dessert and surprise them with it. Cooking something yourself adds a personal touch.

Memory Lane:

- Create a photo album or a collage of memories you've shared together. Present it as a surprise keepsake.

Unexpected Compliment:

- Compliment the person unexpectedly, highlighting something specific that you appreciate about them.

Spur-of-the-Moment Trip:

- Plan a spontaneous day trip or weekend getaway. Surprise them with the destination and the adventure.

Tech-Free Time:

- Declare a tech-free time where you both disconnect from devices and spend quality time together.

Surprise Celebration:

- Organize a surprise celebration for a personal achievement or milestone, even if it's small.

Book or Movie Night:

- Choose a book or movie you think the person will enjoy and organize an impromptu book or movie night.

Help with a Task:

- Offer to help with a task or chore they've been putting off, showing that you care about their well-being.

The key to a successful surprise gesture is thoughtfulness and consideration for the person's preferences and personality. It's about making them feel appreciated and bringing joy to their day.

Planning unexpected date nights

Planning unexpected date nights can add excitement and spontaneity to your relationship. Here are some creative and unexpected date night ideas to surprise your partner:

Indoor Picnic:

- Set up a cozy indoor picnic with blankets, pillows, and your partner's favorite snacks. You can even cook or order a special meal to enjoy together.

Scavenger Hunt:

- Plan a scavenger hunt with clues leading to different locations that are significant to your relationship. It could be places you've been together or places that hold special memories.

Themed Movie Night:

- Choose a theme for your movie night and pick movies, snacks, and decorations that match the theme. For example, you could have a retro movie night, or a night dedicated to your favorite film genre.

Stargazing Adventure:

- Take your partner for a surprise stargazing adventure. Find a quiet spot away from city lights, bring a blanket, and enjoy the beauty of the night sky together.

Cooking Class at Home:

- Sign up for a virtual cooking class or choose a new recipe to try together at home. It's a fun and interactive way to bond while creating a delicious meal.

Escape Room at Home:

- Create your own DIY escape room with puzzles and challenges. Set it up at home and see if you can solve the mystery together.

Art Night:

- Get creative with an art night at home. Set up a canvas, gather some paints, and create your own masterpieces. It's a great way to express yourselves and have fun together.

Outdoor Adventure:

- Plan a surprise outdoor adventure, like a hiking trip, a bike ride, or a day at the beach. Pack a picnic and enjoy the day exploring nature together.

Concert in the Living Room:

- Bring the concert experience home by creating a playlist of your favorite songs, dimming the lights, and having a dance party in the living room.

Bookstore or Library Date:

- Spend an evening at a bookstore or library, exploring new books together. You can take turns picking out books for each other or find a cozy corner to read together.

To consider your partner's interests and preferences when planning a surprise date. The key is to make it personal and tailored to your relationship for a truly memorable experience.

Thoughtful gifts and gestures

Thoughtful gifts and gestures can make a significant impact, showing someone that you care and appreciate them. Here are some ideas for thoughtful gifts and gestures:

1. Personalized Items:

- Customized jewelry with their initials or a special date.
- Personalized photo albums or scrapbooks.
- Custom artwork or a framed photo of a meaningful moment.

2. Acts of Service:

- Offer to run errands or help with tasks they find challenging.

- Cook a homemade meal or organize a surprise dinner.

- Babysit or pet-sit to give them a break.

3. Handwritten Notes:

- Write a heartfelt letter expressing your feelings and appreciation.

- Create a jar of positive notes for them to read when they need a pick-me-up.

- Send postcards or letters in the mail.

4. Memory Lane:

- Compile a playlist of songs that hold special memories.

- Create a photo collage or a digital slideshow.

- Plan a day to revisit meaningful places together.

5. Subscription Services:

- Subscribe them to a magazine or a service aligned with their interests.

- Gift a streaming service, book club, or a wine-of-the-month club.

6. Self-Care Packages:

- Put together a spa day basket with bath salts, candles, and skincare items.

- Gift a relaxation kit with a cozy blanket, a good book, and some tea.

- Create a custom self-care package tailored to their preferences.

7. Learning Experiences:

- Enroll them in a workshop or class for something they've always wanted to learn.

- Plan a day of activities related to a shared interest.

8. Random Acts of Kindness:

- Surprise them with breakfast in bed.

- Leave sticky notes with affirmations in places they'll find throughout the day.

- Randomly send flowers or a small gift to their workplace.

9. Technology and Gadgets:

- Gift a device or accessory that complements their hobbies or work.

- Set up a virtual movie night or game night with friends.

10. Green Gifts:

- Give a potted plant or a small indoor garden.

- Donate to a charity or cause they care about in their name.

11. Hobby-Related Items:

- Purchase tools or accessories for their favorite hobby.

- Book tickets to a concert, play, or sports event they'd enjoy.

12. Time Together:

- Plan a surprise weekend getaway.

- Schedule a day for activities you can enjoy together.

The most meaningful gifts come from knowing the person well and tailoring the gesture to their preferences and needs.

Expressing desires and fantasies

Expressing desires and fantasies is a personal and often intimate aspect of communication. It's important to approach this with respect and sensitivity, especially considering the comfort level and boundaries of the person you are communicating with. Here are some general tips on expressing desires and fantasies:

Establish Trust:

- Before sharing intimate desires or fantasies, ensure there is a foundation of trust in your relationship. This creates a safe space for open communication.

Choose the Right Time and Place:

- Find a suitable and private environment to discuss such matters. Timing is crucial; make sure both of you are relaxed and open to the conversation.

Start Slowly:

- Begin with subtle hints or compliments. Gauge the other person's response and gradually progress to more explicit expressions if the comfort level is reciprocated.

Use Positive Language:

- Frame your desires or fantasies in a positive and affirming manner. Avoid making the other person feel pressured or uncomfortable. Express what you appreciate about the relationship and how these desires can enhance the connection.

Be Specific and Honest:

- Clearly articulate your desires or fantasies without being vague. Honesty is important, but it's equally crucial to be sensitive to the other person's feelings.

Encourage Communication:

- Create an atmosphere where the other person feels comfortable sharing their desires and fantasies as well. This promotes mutual understanding and connection.

Respect Boundaries:

- Understand that not everyone shares the same level of comfort or interest in certain fantasies. Be respectful if the other person expresses discomfort or reluctance.

Discuss Consent:

- If your desires involve any activities that could be considered outside the norm, ensure that there is clear communication and consent from both parties. Respect each other's boundaries and limits.

Consider Non-Verbal Communication:

- Sometimes, non-verbal cues can be just as effective. Pay attention to body language and responses to gauge the other person's comfort level.

Be Open to Compromise:

- Understand that both individuals in a relationship may have different desires and fantasies. Be open to finding common ground and compromise when necessary.

Remember that communication is a two-way street, and maintaining open and honest dialogue is essential for a healthy relationship. Always prioritize consent, respect, and the well-being of both parties involved.

Creating a safe space for open conversation

Creating a safe space for open conversation is crucial for fostering a positive and inclusive environment. Here are some guidelines and tips to help you establish such a space:

Establish Ground Rules:

- Clearly define the purpose of the space.

- Set ground rules for respectful communication.

- Encourage participants to actively listen to each other.

- Emphasize the importance of empathy and understanding.

Encourage Inclusivity:

- Promote diversity and inclusion in the group.

- Acknowledge and respect different perspectives.

- Create an atmosphere where everyone feels welcome and valued.

Ensure Confidentiality:

- Emphasize the confidentiality of discussions.

- Make it clear that personal information shared should remain within the group.

Moderate Effectively:

- Have a neutral moderator who ensures the conversation stays on track.

- Intervene if conversations become disrespectful or offensive.

- Encourage participants to express themselves but in a constructive manner.

Use Inclusive Language:

- Promote the use of inclusive and respectful language.

- Discourage offensive language, slurs, or derogatory remarks.

Provide Trigger Warnings:

- If discussions may cover sensitive topics, provide trigger warnings.

- Allow participants to opt-out of certain discussions if they feel uncomfortable.

Create a Welcoming Physical/Virtual Environment:

- Choose a physical location that is comfortable and private, if applicable.

- For virtual spaces, use platforms that allow for easy communication and are accessible to all participants.

Encourage Open-mindedness:

- Foster an environment where participants are open to changing their perspectives.

- Emphasize the value of learning from each other.

Address Conflicts Promptly:

- Deal with conflicts as soon as they arise.

- Encourage participants to express concerns and find resolution together.

Seek Feedback:

- Regularly ask for feedback on the group dynamics.

- Adjust the guidelines and rules based on the feedback received.

Educate Participants:

- Provide resources or information to educate participants about different perspectives.

- Encourage continuous learning and self-awareness.

Model the Behavior:

- Demonstrate the behavior you want to see in others.

- Be open, respectful, and empathetic in your communication.

Remember that creating a safe space is an ongoing process that requires continuous effort and feedback. Regularly assess the effectiveness of the guidelines and be willing to adapt them as needed to ensure a positive and inclusive environment for open conversation.

Chapter 14

LONG-TERM STRATEGIES FOR SUSTAINING PASSION

Sustaining passion over the long term requires a combination of self-awareness, goal setting, resilience, and continuous learning. Here are some strategies to help you maintain and nurture your passion over time:

Define Your Purpose:

- Clearly articulate why your passion matters to you. Understand the underlying values and motivations that drive your interest.

Set Realistic Goals:

- Break down your passion into achievable short-term and long-term goals. This helps you stay focused and provides a sense of accomplishment along the way.

Create a Roadmap:

- Develop a strategic plan for pursuing your passion. Identify milestones and create a roadmap to guide your progress. This can help you stay organized and maintain a sense of direction.

Embrace Challenges:

- View challenges as opportunities for growth rather than obstacles. Embracing difficulties and setbacks can strengthen your commitment and resilience.

Diversify Your Experience:

- Explore different aspects of your passion to keep it fresh and exciting. This can prevent burnout and provide new perspectives that reignite your enthusiasm.

Balance and Boundaries:

- Maintain a balance between your passion and other aspects of your life, such as work, relationships, and self-care. Establish healthy boundaries to prevent overwhelm.

Continuous Learning:

- Stay curious and committed to learning. As you deepen your knowledge, you'll likely find new layers of your passion that keep it interesting and evolving.

Connect with Like-Minded Individuals:

- Surround yourself with people who share your passion. Engaging with a community can provide support, inspiration, and valuable insights.

Celebrate Achievements:

- Acknowledge and celebrate your accomplishments, both big and small. Recognizing your progress can boost motivation and reinforce your commitment.

Adaptability:

- Be open to adapting your approach and goals as circumstances change. Flexibility is crucial for long-term sustainability.

Mindfulness and Reflection:

- Regularly reflect on your journey and assess how your passion aligns with your values and aspirations. Mindfulness practices can help you stay connected to the present moment.

Self-Care:

- Take care of your physical and mental well-being. Ensure you get enough rest, exercise, and relaxation to maintain the energy and focus needed for pursuing your passion.

Delegate and Seek Support:

- Don't be afraid to delegate tasks or seek support when needed. This can prevent burnout and allow you to focus on the aspects of your passion that truly bring you joy.

Experiment and Innovate:

- Allow room for experimentation and innovation within your passion. This can prevent monotony and keep the experience dynamic.

Remember that sustaining passion is a dynamic process that requires ongoing effort and adaptation. By incorporating these strategies, you can build a foundation for a fulfilling and enduring connection to your interests.

Regular relationship check-ins

Regular relationship check-ins are a valuable practice that can contribute to the health and success of a relationship. These check-ins involve open and honest communication between partners to assess the state of the relationship, address any concerns or issues, and ensure that both individuals are on the same page. Here are some tips on how to conduct effective relationship check-ins:

Schedule Regular Check-Ins:

- Establish a routine for check-ins, whether it's weekly, bi-weekly, or monthly. Consistency helps create a sense of regularity and predictability.

Create a Safe and Comfortable Environment:

- Choose a quiet and comfortable space where you both feel at ease to discuss your feelings openly and honestly.

Use "I" Statements:

- Express your thoughts and feelings using "I" statements to avoid sounding accusatory. For example, say "I feel" instead of "You always" to prevent the conversation from becoming confrontational.

Active Listening:

- Practice active listening by giving your partner your full attention. Repeat back what you've heard to ensure you understand each other.

Share Positives and Concerns:

- Discuss positive aspects of the relationship, as well as any concerns or issues that may have arisen. Acknowledge the things that are going well and express gratitude.

Be Specific:

- When discussing concerns or issues, be specific about what is bothering you. Avoid generalizations and provide examples to help your partner understand your perspective.

Set Goals Together:

- Discuss your individual and shared goals. This can include short-term and long-term goals for the relationship, as well as personal aspirations.

Check-in on Previous Issues:

- If you've discussed specific issues in previous check-ins, follow up on the progress. This shows commitment to resolving problems and working together for the betterment of the relationship.

Be Open to Feedback:

- Be open to receiving feedback from your partner and be willing to make adjustments if necessary. Constructive feedback can be valuable for personal and relationship growth.

Celebrate Achievements:

- Take time to celebrate the achievements and milestones you've reached as a couple. This can strengthen your bond and create positive reinforcement.

Remember that effective communication is key in any relationship. Regular check-ins help build trust, enhance understanding, and foster a healthy and supportive connection between partners.

Assessing progress

Assessing progress can be approached in various ways depending on the context, whether it's personal development, project management, or organizational growth. Here are some general strategies you can use:

Define Clear Goals:

Clearly define your goals and objectives. Ensure that they are specific, measurable, achievable, relevant, and time-bound (SMART).

Regular Check-Ins:

- Schedule regular check-ins to review progress. This could be daily, weekly, monthly, or based on the timeline of your project or goals.

Key Performance Indicators (KPIs):

- Identify and monitor key performance indicators relevant to your goals. These could include metrics like sales numbers, completion rates, customer satisfaction, etc.

Data Analysis:

- Collect and analyze relevant data. This could involve looking at financial reports, customer feedback, user engagement metrics, or any other data that provides insights into your progress.

Feedback Mechanism:

- Establish a feedback mechanism. Gather feedback from team members, stakeholders, or mentors to gain different perspectives on your progress.

Adjustment and Adaptation:

- Be willing to adapt your strategies based on the feedback and data analysis. If something is not working, consider making changes or trying a different approach.

Celebrate Milestones:

- Acknowledge and celebrate achievements along the way. This helps boost morale and motivation.

SWOT Analysis:

- Conduct a SWOT (Strengths, Weaknesses, Opportunities, Threats) analysis to assess internal and external factors that may impact your progress.

Time Management:

- Evaluate how well you are managing your time. Ensure that you are allocating resources effectively and staying on schedule.

Reflect on Learning:

- Reflect on what you've learned during the process. Understanding both successes and failures can provide valuable insights for future endeavors.

Documentation:

- Keep records of your progress. This documentation can be useful for future reference and for analyzing the journey you've taken.

Peer Review:

- Seek input from peers or mentors. They may provide valuable perspectives and advice that can help you assess your progress more accurately.

Continuous Improvement:

- Embrace a mindset of continuous improvement. Always look for ways to enhance processes, skills, and overall performance.

Remember that progress assessment is an ongoing and dynamic process. It requires a combination of objective data analysis, self-reflection, and a willingness to adapt to changing circumstances.

Adjusting strategies as needed

Adjusting strategies as needed is a critical aspect of decision-making and problem-solving in various contexts, such as business, personal development, and project management. Here are some general guidelines on how to effectively adjust strategies:

Regular Evaluation:

- Regularly assess the progress and outcomes of your current strategy.

- Identify key performance indicators (KPIs) and measure them to gauge success.

- Determine if the initial assumptions and conditions have changed.

Flexibility:

- Acknowledge that circumstances can change, and a strategy that worked in the past may not be as effective in the present.

- Be open to adapting your approach based on new information and changing conditions.

Continuous Monitoring:

- Set up a system for continuous monitoring of relevant factors and variables.

- Stay informed about industry trends, market conditions, and any external factors that may impact your strategy.

Feedback Mechanisms:

- Establish feedback mechanisms to gather insights from stakeholders, team members, or customers.

- Act on constructive feedback and use it to refine or modify your strategy.

Scenario Planning:

- Anticipate potential scenarios and develop contingency plans.

- Consider best-case, worst-case, and most likely scenarios to prepare for a range of possibilities.

Risk Management:

- Regularly assess risks associated with your strategy.

- Develop risk mitigation plans to address potential challenges.

Communication:

- Maintain open communication channels with team members, stakeholders, and relevant parties.

- Ensure that everyone involved is aware of changes in strategy and understands the reasons behind them.

Data-Driven Decision Making:

- Base your decisions on data and analytics when possible.

- Use key metrics and data to guide adjustments to your strategy.

Agility:

- Embrace an agile mindset that allows for quick adaptation to changing circumstances.

- Break down larger strategies into smaller, manageable tasks with shorter feedback loops.

Learn from Mistakes:

- If a strategy is not yielding the expected results, analyze the reasons behind it.

- Learn from mistakes and use them as opportunities for improvement.

Benchmarking:

- Compare your strategy and its outcomes to industry benchmarks and best practices.

- Identify areas where you can learn from others and make adjustments accordingly.

The ability to adjust strategies as needed is a valuable skill, and it often involves a combination of analytical thinking, creativity, and a willingness to embrace change.

Continuous communication and adaptation

Continuous communication and adaptation are crucial principles in various aspects of life, from personal relationships to business strategies and technological developments. Here's a breakdown of these concepts:

Continuous Communication:

- In Relationships: Effective communication is the foundation of healthy relationships. Regular and open communication helps build trust, understanding, and intimacy. It allows individuals to express their thoughts, feelings, and needs while also being receptive to others.

- In Business: Within organizations, continuous communication fosters collaboration, teamwork, and a shared sense of purpose. Regular updates, team meetings, and feedback sessions help align employees with organizational goals and ensure everyone is on the same page.

- In Technology: In the context of technology and software development, continuous communication is essential for agile methodologies. Teams frequently communicate updates, challenges, and progress to adapt quickly to changing requirements and deliver high-quality products.

Adaptation:

- In Personal Growth: Life is dynamic, and individuals need to adapt to changing circumstances. This might involve learning new skills, adjusting to different environments, or evolving personal perspectives. Embracing change and being flexible are key aspects of personal growth.

- In Business Strategies: In the business world, adaptability is a critical trait for success. Markets evolve, customer preferences change, and technology advances. Companies that can adapt their strategies, products, and services in response to these changes are more likely to thrive in a competitive landscape.

- In Technology and Innovation: The tech industry thrives on adaptation. Continuous advancements and innovations require quick adaptation to new technologies and methodologies. This is evident in fields like artificial intelligence, where rapid changes and breakthroughs occur regularly.

Synergy of Continuous Communication and Adaptation:

- Combining continuous communication with adaptation is powerful. Open lines of communication facilitate the exchange of ideas, feedback, and information necessary for informed decision-making.

- When teams communicate effectively, they can adapt to challenges and opportunities more readily. The ability to learn from experiences, iterate on processes, and adjust strategies based on feedback is a hallmark of successful and dynamic individuals, teams, and organizations.

Embracing continuous communication and adaptation is fundamental for personal growth, successful relationships, thriving businesses, and staying relevant in rapidly changing environments. The synergy of these principles enables individuals and entities to navigate uncertainties and capitalize on new opportunities.

Remaining open to change

Remaining open to change is a valuable mindset and approach in various aspects of life, including personal development, relationships, and professional endeavors. Here are some reasons why staying open to change is important:

- Adaptability: The ability to adapt to new circumstances and embrace change is crucial in a world that is constantly evolving. Being open to change allows you to adjust your mindset, behaviors, and strategies to better navigate new situations.

- Learning and Growth: Change often brings new opportunities for learning and personal growth. By staying open to change, you can embrace challenges as chances to acquire new skills, knowledge, and experiences.

- Innovation: Change is often a catalyst for innovation. Whether in the workplace or in personal projects, being open to change can lead to creative solutions, improvements, and the development of novel ideas.

- Resilience: Resilience is the ability to bounce back from setbacks. When you're open to change, you are better equipped to face challenges and setbacks with a positive mindset, finding ways to overcome obstacles and move forward.

- Improved Problem-Solving: Change often presents new problems to solve. Being open to change encourages a flexible and open-minded approach to problem-solving, enabling you to think outside the box and find effective solutions.

- Enhanced Interpersonal Relationships: In personal relationships, being open to change is essential for growth and understanding. People change over time, and being receptive to those changes can strengthen relationships by fostering empathy, communication, and mutual support.

- Career Advancement: In the professional realm, being open to change is often associated with a willingness to learn, adapt, and take on new responsibilities. This can contribute to career advancement, as employers value individuals who are flexible and can thrive in dynamic environments.

- Reduced Stress: Resisting change can lead to stress and anxiety, as it creates tension between what is and what could be. Embracing change with an open mind can reduce stress by promoting a more positive and proactive approach to the uncertainties of life.

- Increased Creativity: Change can stimulate creativity by breaking routines and introducing new perspectives. Embracing change allows for the exploration of different ideas and approaches, fostering a more creative and innovative mindset.

- Personal Satisfaction: Embracing change often leads to a sense of accomplishment and personal satisfaction. It demonstrates your ability to overcome challenges, adapt to new circumstances, and proactively shape your life.

While staying open to change is important, it's also crucial to strike a balance and recognize when certain principles or values should remain constant. Being discerning about the types of changes you embrace ensures that you maintain a sense of authenticity and stability while still adapting to the dynamic nature of life.

Growing together as a couple

Growing together as a couple is a dynamic and ongoing process that involves both individuals making conscious efforts to strengthen their relationship. Here are some key principles and suggestions to foster growth in your relationship:

- Communication: Open and honest communication is the foundation of any strong relationship. Share your thoughts, feelings, and concerns with your partner regularly. Be a good listener and show empathy.

- Quality Time: Spend quality time together regularly. This doesn't always have to be extravagant; even simple activities like cooking together, taking a walk, or having a meaningful conversation can strengthen your bond.

- Shared Goals and Values: Discuss your individual goals, both short-term and long-term. Identify common values and aspirations and work together to align your life paths. Having shared goals creates a sense of unity and purpose.

- Mutual Respect: Respect is crucial in any relationship. Acknowledge and appreciate each other's differences and treat each other with kindness and consideration. Respect also involves supporting each other's personal growth.

- Adaptability: Life is full of changes and challenges. Being adaptable as a couple helps you navigate these changes together. Be open to compromise and find solutions that work for both of you.

- Individual Growth: While growing together is important, it's also crucial to support each other's individual growth. Encourage your partner to pursue their passions and personal development and do the same for yourself.

- Conflict Resolution: Disagreements are a natural part of any relationship. Learn healthy ways to resolve conflicts, focusing on understanding each other's perspectives rather than trying to "win" an argument.

- Celebrate Achievements: Acknowledge and celebrate each other's successes, whether big or small. This helps build a positive and supportive environment in your relationship.

- Continual Learning: Be curious about each other and continue to learn about your partner. People evolve over time, and staying connected requires ongoing effort to understand and appreciate the changes.

- Physical Intimacy: Physical connection is an important aspect of a romantic relationship. Keep the flame alive through affection, intimacy, and regular expressions of love.

- Surprises and Spontaneity: Keep the relationship exciting by introducing surprises and spontaneity. It could be as simple as planning a surprise date or trying new activities together.

Remember that each relationship is unique, and what works for one couple may not work for another. The key is to be attentive, responsive, and committed to the well-being and growth of both individuals and the relationship as a whole.

Chapter 15
MAINTAINING LONG-TERM SUCCESS

Maintaining long-term success involves a combination of strategic planning, consistent effort, adaptability, and a focus on personal and professional development. Here are some key principles and tips to help you achieve and sustain long-term success:

Set Clear Goals:

- Define your short-term and long-term goals clearly.

- Break down larger goals into smaller, manageable tasks.

Consistent Effort:

- Success often requires persistent and consistent effort over time.

- Develop good habits and routines that support your goals.

Adaptability:

- Be open to change and adapt to evolving circumstances.

- Learn from failures and use them as opportunities for growth.

Continuous Learning:

- Stay curious and committed to lifelong learning.

- Regularly update your skills and knowledge to stay relevant.

Time Management:

- Prioritize tasks based on importance and deadlines.

- Avoid procrastination and use your time efficiently.

Build Strong Relationships:

- Cultivate positive and supportive relationships personally and professionally.

- Networking and collaboration can lead to new opportunities.

Embrace Challenges:

- See challenges as opportunities to learn and grow.

- Develop a positive mindset and resilience in the face of setbacks.

Financial Management:

- Make informed financial decisions and save for the future.

- Be mindful of spending and invest wisely.

Wellness and Work-Life Balance:

- Take care of your physical and mental well-being.

- Maintain a healthy work-life balance to prevent burnout.

Leadership Skills:

- Develop leadership qualities, even if you're not in a formal leadership position.

- Lead by example and inspire others to achieve their best.

Adopt a Growth Mindset:

- Believe in your ability to learn and improve.

- View challenges as opportunities to develop rather than as threats.

Celebrate Achievements:

- Acknowledge and celebrate both small and large achievements.

- Reflect on your progress regularly.

Give Back:

- Contribute to your community or industry.

- Volunteer and share your knowledge and skills with others.

Stay Current:

- Keep up with industry trends and advancements.

- Anticipate changes and position yourself to leverage new opportunities.

Regular Self-Reflection:

- Take time to reflect on your goals, values, and progress.

- Adjust your plans and strategies as needed.

Remember that long-term success is a journey, not a destination. It requires ongoing commitment, self-awareness, and a willingness to adapt to the changing landscape of your personal and professional life.

Building a resilient relationship

Building a resilient relationship is essential for its long-term success and ability to withstand challenges. Resilient relationships are characterized by mutual support, effective communication, and the ability to navigate difficulties together. Here are some key principles to help you build resilience in your relationship:

Effective Communication:

- Open and Honest Communication: Foster an environment where both partners feel comfortable expressing their thoughts and feelings without fear of judgment.

- Active Listening: Practice active listening to truly understand your partner's perspective. Repeat what you've heard to ensure clarity and show that you are engaged.

Mutual Respect:

- Valuing Differences: Recognize and appreciate each other's individuality, including differences in opinions, values, and interests.

- Positive Regard: Treat your partner with kindness and respect, even in moments of disagreement. Focus on the positive aspects of your partner and the relationship.

Emotional Support:

- Empathy: Try to understand and validate your partner's emotions, even if you don't agree with them. Empathy builds a strong emotional connection.

- Being Present: Be there for your partner in times of need, offering comfort and support. Show that you are a reliable source of emotional support.

Adaptability:

- Flexibility: Recognize that life is unpredictable, and circumstances may change. Be open to adapting your plans and expectations as needed.

- Problem-Solving: Approach challenges as a team. Work together to find solutions to problems, focusing on the issue at hand rather than blaming each other.

Shared Goals and Values:

- Common Objectives: Identify and work towards shared goals that align with both partners' values. This creates a sense of unity and purpose in the relationship.

- Long-Term Vision: Discuss your vision for the future together and ensure that you are both on the same page regarding major life decisions.

Quality Time:

- Spending Time Together: Dedicate quality time to nurture your connection. This could be through shared activities, date nights, or simply spending time talking and enjoying each other's company.

- Balance Independence and Togetherness: Allow each other space for personal growth and individual pursuits while maintaining a strong connection.

Conflict Resolution:

- Constructive Conflict: Learn how to navigate disagreements in a healthy way. Focus on the issue, not personal attacks, and work towards finding a resolution that satisfies both partners.

- Apologize and Forgive: Apologize when necessary and forgive each other. Holding onto resentment can erode the foundation of a resilient relationship.

Continuous Growth:

- Individual and Relationship Growth: Encourage personal growth and support each other's aspirations. A resilient relationship is one where both partners evolve and grow together.

Remember that building resilience is an ongoing process that requires commitment and effort from both partners. Regularly check in with each other, assess the health of your relationship, and make adjustments as needed to keep it strong and resilient.

Continuous effort and commitment

Continuous effort and commitment are key factors that contribute to personal and professional success. Whether you are pursuing a goal, working on a project, or striving for self-improvement, maintaining a consistent level of effort and commitment is essential. Here's why these two aspects are crucial:

Achieving Goals:

- Consistent Progress: Continuous effort ensures that you make steady progress toward your goals. Small, consistent steps over time can lead to significant achievements.

- Overcoming Challenges: Commitment helps you persevere through challenges and setbacks. It provides the resilience needed to navigate obstacles and stay focused on your objectives.

Skill Development:

- Mastery: Consistent effort is necessary for skill development and mastery in any field. Regular practice and learning contribute to continuous improvement.

- Adaptability: Commitment allows you to adapt to changing circumstances and learn from experiences. It helps you stay open to new ideas and approaches.

Building Habits:

- Establishing Routines: Continuous effort is essential for forming positive habits. Whether it's a daily routine for personal well-being or work habits for increased productivity, commitment is crucial for habit formation.

- Behavioral Change: Commitment is the driving force behind behavior change. It helps you replace old habits with new, more constructive ones.

Professional Success:

- Career Advancement: A strong work ethic and commitment to excellence contribute to professional success. Employers value employees who consistently deliver high-quality work and are committed to their roles.

- Leadership: Leaders often demonstrate unwavering commitment, inspiring and motivating others to follow suit.

Personal Growth:

- Self-Discipline: Continuous effort and commitment require self-discipline. This quality is fundamental for personal growth, enabling you to overcome procrastination and distractions.

- Resilience: Commitment fosters resilience, helping you bounce back from failures and setbacks. It encourages a positive mindset even in challenging situations.

Long-Term Success:

- Endurance: Long-term success often requires endurance. Continuous effort and commitment sustain your momentum over the long haul, preventing burnout and fostering a sense of fulfillment.

Continuous effort and commitment are the cornerstones of achievement and personal development. They provide the fuel needed to navigate the journey toward your goals, overcome obstacles, and realize lasting success.

Adapting to changes and challenges

Adapting to changes and challenges is a crucial skill that allows individuals and organizations to thrive in a dynamic and uncertain world. Here are some strategies to help you navigate and adapt effectively.

Cultivate a Growth Mindset:

- Embrace challenges as opportunities for learning and growth.

- View failures as opportunities to improve rather than as setbacks.

- Believe in your ability to develop new skills and overcome obstacles.

Stay Agile:

- Be open to change and proactively seek ways to improve.

- Stay flexible in your approach and be willing to adjust plans as needed.

- Continuously reassess and realign goals with changing circumstances.

Build Resilience:

- Develop emotional resilience to bounce back from setbacks.

- Focus on building a strong support system of friends, family, and colleagues.

- Practice stress-reduction techniques such as mindfulness and meditation.

Continuous Learning:

- Stay curious and be committed to lifelong learning.

- Acquire new skills and stay updated on industry trends.

- Seek feedback and be open to constructive criticism as a means of personal and professional development.

Adaptability:

- Be open to new ideas and perspectives.

- Demonstrate a willingness to adapt your thinking and strategies.

- Foster a culture of adaptability within teams and organizations.

Effective Communication:

- Communicate openly and transparently about changes and challenges.

- Encourage feedback and create a culture where ideas can be freely exchanged.

- Ensure that everyone is on the same page and understands the reasons behind changes.

Problem-Solving Skills:

- Develop strong problem-solving skills to address challenges systematically.

- Break down complex problems into smaller, more manageable components.

- Collaborate with others to generate creative solutions.

Time Management:

- Prioritize tasks and focus on high-impact activities.

- Be adaptable in managing your time and priorities based on changing circumstances.

- Delegate tasks when appropriate to maximize efficiency.

Networking and Collaboration:

- Build a diverse network of professionals to exchange ideas and perspectives.

- Collaborate with others to leverage collective strengths.

- Seek partnerships and alliances that can help navigate challenges more effectively.

Strategic Planning:

- Develop a clear vision and long-term goals.

- Regularly review and adjust strategic plans in response to changing environments.

- Anticipate potential challenges and plan for contingencies.

Remember that adaptability is a skill that can be developed over time. Embrace change as a constant and use each experience as an opportunity for personal and professional growth.

Final thoughts and encouragement

Building and maintaining meaningful connections is a lifelong journey that requires effort, understanding, and genuine care. As you embark on this path, here are some final thoughts and words of encouragement:

Invest Time and Energy:

- Building strong connections takes time and energy. It's an investment in your personal and professional well-being. Be patient and persistent.

Quality Over Quantity:

- Focus on the quality of your connections rather than the quantity. A few deep, meaningful relationships often bring more fulfillment than a large number of superficial ones.

Embrace Diversity:

- Celebrate diversity in your connections. Embrace different perspectives, backgrounds, and experiences. Diversity enriches relationships and broadens your horizons.

Learn and Grow Together:

- Relationships provide opportunities for mutual learning and growth. Embrace challenges as opportunities for personal and collective development.

Express Gratitude:

- Take the time to express gratitude for the people in your life. Acknowledge their contributions and the positive impact they've had on you. Gratitude strengthens connections.

Stay Positive in Challenges:

- Challenges are inevitable in any relationship. Approach difficulties with a positive mindset, viewing them as opportunities to strengthen the bond and find solutions together.

Celebrate Milestones:

- Celebrate the successes and milestones, both big and small. Acknowledge achievements and special moments, as they contribute to the overall positive atmosphere of the relationship.

Be Authentic:

- Be true to yourself in your relationships. Authenticity fosters trust and deepens connections. Let others see and appreciate the real you.

Forgive and Let Go:

- Forgiveness is a powerful tool in maintaining relationships. Learn to forgive, let go of grudges, and focus on moving forward together.

Nurture Self-Compassion:

- Be compassionate with yourself. Understand that you, too, are a work in progress. Practice self-care and self-compassion, as a healthy relationship with yourself positively impacts your connections with others.

Remember that building connections is not about perfection but about progress. Every interaction, positive or challenging, contributes to the growth and depth of your relationships. Cherish the connections you have, and approach new ones with an open heart. The journey of cultivating ongoing connections is a fulfilling and enriching one, and your efforts will be rewarded with a network of people who truly matter in your life.

Author Summary
WELLNESS WHISPERER

In the world of relationship and parenting guides, a guiding voice emerges under the pen name "Wellness Whisperer." Meet the man behind the wisdom, a dedicated father of three, passionate about fostering healthy connections within families. As a parent who has weathered the storms and relished the joys of raising a family, the Wellness Whisperer shares insights garnered from the trenches of parenthood, delivering a unique blend of warmth, wisdom, and practical advice.

Despite his personal and family-oriented approach, the Wellness Whisperer maintains a certain air of mystery, choosing to let his words speak louder than his identity. Drawing from his experiences as a father, he crafts guides that resonate with the challenges and triumphs of modern family life.

As the Wellness Whisperer, our author prioritizes the well-being of both parents and children, recognizing the symbiotic relationship between parental happiness and a thriving family dynamic. His writing reflects a deep understanding of the intricate dance between partners and the delicate balance required in nurturing the growth of each family member.

With a focus on fostering emotional intelligence, effective communication, and meaningful connections, the Wellness Whisperer offers a refreshing perspective in the often complex landscape of relationships and parenting. His commitment to guiding readers towards healthier family dynamics is evident in the empathy woven into every word.

While the Wellness Whisperer is not afraid to explore the challenges of parenting, he approaches them with a positive and solution-oriented mindset. Rooted in authenticity and a genuine desire to help families flourish, his advice is not prescriptive but rather an invitation to embark on a journey of self-discovery and growth.

For those seeking a compassionate, insightful guide through the maze of modern family life, the Wellness Whisperer's work promises to be a source of inspiration and practical wisdom. Join him on a journey towards building stronger, more fulfilling relationships and creating a nurturing environment where both parents and children can thrive. The Wellness Whisperer is more than a pen name; it's an embodiment of a guiding presence committed to the wellness of your family's heart and soul.